ISADORA DUNCAN

ISADORA DUNCAN

RUTH KOZODOY

CHELSEA HOUSE PUBLISHERS

NEW YORK • PHILADELPHIA

EDITOR–IN–CHIEF: Nancy Toff
EXECUTIVE EDITOR: Remmel T. Nunn
MANAGING EDITOR: Karyn Gullen Browne
COPY CHIEF: Juliann Barbato
PICTURE EDITOR: Adrian G. Allen
ART DIRECTOR: Giannella Garrett
MANUFACTURING MANAGER: Gerald Levine

Staff for ISADORA DUNCAN:

SENIOR EDITOR: Constance Jones
TEXT EDITOR: Marian W. Taylor
ASSISTANT EDITOR: Maria Behan
COPYEDITOR: Ellen Scordato
EDITORIAL ASSISTANT: Theodore Keyes
PICTURE RESEARCHER: Lisa Kirschner
DESIGNER: Design Oasis
PRODUCTION COORDINATOR: Joseph Romano
COVER ILLUSTRATION: Richard Leonard

3 5 7 9 8 6 4

Library of Congress Cataloging in Publication Data

Kozodoy, Ruth. ISADORA DUNCAN

(American women of achievement)
Bibliography: p.
Includes index.
1. Duncan, Isadora, 1878–1927. 2. Dancers
—United States—Biography. I. Title. II. Series
GV1785.D8K69 1988   793.3′2′0924 [B]   87-17865

ISBN 1-55546-650-8
    0-7910-0414-7 (pbk.)

CONTENTS

AMERICAN WOMEN OF ACHIEVEMENT

Abigail Adams
women's rights advocate

Jane Addams
social worker

Louisa May Alcott
author

Marian Anderson
singer

Susan B. Anthony
woman suffragist

Ethel Barrymore
actress

Clara Barton
*founder of the American
Red Cross*

Elizabeth Blackwell
physician

Nellie Bly
journalist

Margaret Bourke-White
photographer

Pearl Buck
author

Rachel Carson
biologist and author

Mary Cassatt
artist

Agnes De Mille
choreographer

Emily Dickinson
poet

Isadora Duncan
dancer

Amelia Earhart
aviator

Mary Baker Eddy
*founder of the Christian
Science church*

Betty Friedan
feminist

Althea Gibson
tennis champion

Emma Goldman
political activist

Helen Hayes
actress

Lillian Hellman
playwright

Katharine Hepburn
actress

Karen Horney
psychoanalyst

Anne Hutchinson
religious leader

Mahalia Jackson
gospel singer

Helen Keller
humanitarian

Jeane Kirkpatrick
diplomat

Emma Lazarus
poet

Clare Boothe Luce
author and diplomat

Barbara McClintock
biologist

Margaret Mead
anthropologist

Edna St. Vincent Millay
poet

Julia Morgan
architect

Grandma Moses
painter

Louise Nevelson
sculptor

Sandra Day O'Connor
Supreme Court justice

Georgia O'Keeffe
painter

Eleanor Roosevelt
diplomat and humanitarian

Wilma Rudolph
champion athlete

Florence Sabin
medical researcher

Beverly Sills
opera singer

Gertrude Stein
author

Gloria Steinem
feminist

Harriet Beecher Stowe
author and abolitionist

Mae West
entertainer

Edith Wharton
author

Phillis Wheatley
poet

Babe Didrikson Zaharias
champion athlete

CHELSEA HOUSE PUBLISHERS

"Remember the Ladies"

MATINA S. HORNER

Remember the Ladies." That is what Abigail Adams wrote to her husband John, then a delegate to the Continental Congress, as the Founding Fathers met in Philadelphia to form a new nation in March of 1776. "Be more generous and favorable to them than your ancestors. Do not put such unlimited power in the hands of the Husbands. If particular care and attention is not paid to the Ladies," Abigail Adams warned, "we are determined to foment a Rebellion, and will not hold ourselves bound by any Laws in which we have no voice, or Representation."

The words of Abigail Adams, one of the earliest American advocates of women's rights, were prophetic. Because when we have not "remembered the ladies," they have, by their words and deeds, reminded us so forcefully of the omission that we cannot fail to remember them. For the history of American women is as interesting and varied as the history of our nation as a whole. American women have played an integral part in founding, settling, and building our country. Some we remember as remarkable women who—against great odds—achieved distinction in the public arena: Anne Hutchinson, who in the 17th century became a charismatic religious leader; Phillis Wheatley, an 18th-century black slave who became a poet; Susan B. Anthony, whose name is synonymous with the 19th-century women's rights movement, and who led the struggle to enfranchise women; and, in our own century, Amelia Earhart, the first woman to cross the Atlantic Ocean by air.

These extraordinary women certainly merit our admiration, but other women, "common women," many of them all but forgotten, should also be recognized for their contributions to American thought and culture. Women have been community builders; they have founded schools and formed voluntary associations to help those in need; they have assumed the major responsibility for rearing children, passing on from one generation to the next the values that keep a culture alive. These and innumerable other contributions, once ignored, are now being recognized by scholars, students, and the public. It is exciting and gratifying to realize that a part of our history that was hardly acknowledged a few generations ago is now being studied and brought to light.

In recent decades, the field of women's history has grown from obscurity to a politically controversial splinter movement to academic respectability, in many cases mainstreamed into such traditional disciplines as history, economics, and psychology. Scholars of women, both female and male, have organized research centers at such prestigious institutions as Wellesley College, Stanford University, and the University of California. Other notable centers for women's studies are the Center for the American Woman and Politics at the Eagleton Institute of Politics at Rutgers University, the Henry A. Murray Research Center for the Study of Lives, at Radcliffe College, and the Women's Research and Education Institute, the research arm of the Congressional Caucus on Women's Issues. Other scholars and public figures have established archives and libraries, such as the Schlesinger Library on the History of Women in America, at Radcliffe College, and the Sophia Smith Collection, at Smith College, to collect and preserve the written and tangible legacies of women.

From the initial donation of the Women's Rights Collection in 1943, the Schlesinger Library grew to encompass vast collections documenting the manifold accomplishments of American women. Simultaneously, the women's movement in general and the academic discipline of women's studies in particular also began with a narrow definition and gradually expanded their mandate. Early causes such as woman suffrage and social reform, abolition and organized labor were joined by newer concerns such as the history of women in business and the professions and in politics and government; the study of the family; and social issues such as health policy and education.

Women, as historian Arthur M. Schlesinger, jr., once pointed out, "have constituted the most spectacular casualty of traditional history. They have made up at least half the human race, but you could never tell that by looking at the books historians write." The new breed of historians is remedying that omission. They have written books about immigrant women and about working-class women who struggled for survival in cities and about black women who met the challenges of life in rural areas. They are telling the stories of women who, despite the barriers of tradition and economics, became lawyers and doctors and public figures.

The women's studies movement has also led scholars to question traditional interpretations of their respective disciplines. For example, the study of war has traditionally been an exercise in military and political analysis, an examination of strategies planned and executed by men. But scholars of women's history have pointed out that wars have also been periods of tremendous change and even opportunity for women, because the very absence of men on the home front enabled them to expand their educational, economic, and professional activities and to assume leadership in their homes.

The early scholars of women's history showed a unique brand of courage in choosing to investigate new subjects and take new approaches to old ones. Often, like their subjects, they endured criticism and even ostracism by their academic colleagues. But their efforts have unquestionably been worthwhile, because with the publication of each new study and book another piece of the historical patchwork is sewn into place, revealing an increasingly comprehensive picture of the role of women in our rich and varied history.

Such books on groups of women are essential, but books that focus on the lives of individuals are equally indispensable. Biographies can be inspirational, offering their readers the example of people with vision who have looked outside themselves for their goals and have often struggled against great obstacles to achieve them. Marian Anderson, for instance, had to overcome racial bigotry in order to perfect her art and perform as a concert singer. Isadora Duncan defied the rules of classical dance to find true artistic freedom. Jane Addams had to break down society's notions of the proper role for women in order to create new social institutions, notably the settlement house. All of these women had to come to terms both with themselves and with the world in which they lived. Only then could they move ahead as pioneers in their chosen callings.

Biography can inspire not only by adulation but also by realism. It helps us to see not only the qualities in others that we hope to emulate, but also, perhaps, the weaknesses that made them "human." By helping us identify with the subject on a more personal level they help us to feel that we, too, can achieve such goals. We read about Eleanor Roosevelt, for instance, who occupied a unique and seemingly enviable position as the wife of the president. Yet we can sympathize with her inner dilemma: an inherently shy woman, she had to force herself to live a most public life in order to use her position to benefit others. We may not be able to imagine ourselves having the immense poetic talent of Emily Dickinson, but from her story we can understand the challenges faced by a creative woman who was expected to fulfill many family responsibilities. And though few of us will ever reach the level of athletic accomplishment displayed by Wilma Rudolph or Babe Zaharias, we can still appreciate their spirit, their overwhelming will to excel.

A biography is a multifaceted lens. It is first of all a magnification, the intimate examination of one particular life. But at the same time, it is a wide-angle lens, informing us about the world in which the subject lived. We come away from reading about one life knowing more about the social, political, and economic fabric of the time. It is for this reason, perhaps, that the great New England essayist Ralph Waldo Emerson wrote, in 1841, "There is properly no history: only biography." And it is also why biography, and particularly women's biography, will continue to fascinate writers and readers alike.

ISADORA DUNCAN

Twenty-four-year-old Isadora Duncan, barefoot and wearing her trademark Grecian-style toga, assumes a characteristic stance during her debut at the Berlin Opera House in March 1903.

ONE

Beginnings

Berlin, 1903. The young woman stood alone and silent on the bare stage. Facing her were hundreds of people, swathed in furs and glittering with jewels. The atmosphere crackled with excitement, but the only sound in the vast theater was a subdued, expectant rustle from the audience.

For weeks, Germany's capital had been buzzing with rumors about this young woman, American dancer Isadora Duncan. Everywhere they looked, Berliners had seen posters heralding her appearance; every newspaper they read had been filled with accounts of her almost ecstatic reception in other German cities.

She danced, it was reported, without a partner, without a dance company, without scenery, without ballet slippers—and, some said, almost without clothes. Now, Berliners would find out

for themselves. Everyone who had managed to beg, buy, or steal a ticket was squeezed into the theater, eyes riveted on the stage. The slender, dark-haired woman before them was indeed lightly dressed. Her body was loosely draped in filmy cloth and her feet were bare.

The orchestra began to play and Isadora Duncan began to dance. Her movements seemed to be directed by forces within her, gentle and graceful one moment; stormy, almost violent, the next. She appeared to be overpowered by an emotion so intense that it radiated from her body in waves.

The audience, too, was overpowered. At the end of Duncan's performance, the theater exploded with thunderous applause. Duncan danced one encore, then another. Still, the audience wanted more. When she made it clear that she would dance no longer, hundreds of usually sophisticated, dignified Berliners rushed to the footlights and leaped onto the stage.

Duncan finally made her way to her dressing room, but when she emerged, she was once again engulfed by her admirers. Unhitching the horses from her carriage, they pulled it through the streets themselves, shouting and cheering. Isadora Duncan rode through Berlin at the center of a triumphal procession.

"I took Berlin by storm," noted Duncan later. The flamboyant dancer was occasionally known to exaggerate, but in this case, her remark was an understatement. She had become the new hero of Germany, known as "the divine, the holy Isadora." How had this young American woman acquired the power to attract so many thousands of passionate followers all across Europe?

Angela Isadora Duncan was born on May 27, 1878, the youngest of four children in a prosperous San Francisco family. Her parents, Dora and Joseph, were well educated, energetic, and charming, an apparently happy couple. Soon after Isadora's birth, however, their marriage fell apart.

When Isadora was still a baby, a bank founded by her father was declared bankrupt. Accused of fraud, Joseph Duncan went into hiding. He was eventually tried and found innocent, but by then, his wife—who suspected

him not only of dishonesty but of unfaithfulness—had left him. After her divorce, Dora Duncan found herself with little money and four young children to support. She began to give music lessons, earning just enough to feed and clothe her family. Because she taught in her pupils' homes, she was usually out during the daytime. Left to their own devices, the Duncan children grew up undisciplined and fiercely independent.

Isadora started going to school when she was five years old, but it was not a happy experience. In the late 19th century, even very young children were expected to sit perfectly still during the school day, memorizing and reciting their lessons. To Isadora, these constraints were both irritating and meaningless. Even then, as she said later, she was "already a dancer and a revolutionist."

In her autobiography, *My Life*, she recalled her first Christmas at school. Dora Duncan, a loving but unsentimental mother, made a point of being honest with her children. The young Duncans, therefore, learned early that Santa Claus was a myth. So when the teacher distributed candy to the children, claiming that it came from Santa Claus, "I rose," reported Duncan, "and solemnly replied, 'I don't believe you. There is no such thing as Santa Claus.'"

Clearly annoyed, the teacher told the little girl that the candy was only

Joseph Duncan, Isadora's father, was accused of fraud when his bank failed in 1877. Arrested while trying to flee to Nicaragua on a sailing ship, he was brought to trial but found not guilty.

Dora Duncan "was too busy to think of any dangers which might befall her children," said her daughter Isadora. "Therefore my two brothers and I were free to follow our own vagabond impulses."

for those who *did* believe in Santa Claus. "Then," said Isadora, "I don't want your candy." She turned to her classmates and shouted, "I don't believe lies! My mother told me she is too poor to be Santa Claus; it is only the rich mothers who can pretend to be Santa Claus and give presents."

The teacher punished the rebellious Isadora by making her stand in the corner. But the child kept right on chanting, "There is no Santa Claus, there is no Santa Claus!" Finally, exasperated, the teacher sent her home, still shouting, "There is no Santa

Claus," at the top of her lungs. "I never got over the feeling," she wrote, "of the injustice with which I had been treated, deprived of candy and punished for telling the truth."

When she got home, Isadora asked her mother, "Wasn't I right? There is no Santa Claus, is there?" Of Irish descent, Dora Duncan had been raised as a Catholic, but she had rejected that faith. She had learned to depend on herself to supply life's material necessities, and she believed that each individual's spiritual needs were fulfilled from his own inner strength.

Duncan, shown here at the age of three, firmly believed that the adult personality was formed in childhood. At an early age, she said, "I was already a dancer and a revolutionist."

Her daughter, said Dora Duncan, had been right. "There is no Santa Claus," she told her, "and there is no God, only your own spirit to help you." Maintaining her convictions even under pressure was only one of the lessons Isadora learned from her mother. A highly cultivated woman,

Dora Duncan also taught her children to share her love for music and literature. Isadora had no use for school, but she thoroughly enjoyed her mother's teaching methods. "My real education," she wrote, "came during the evenings when my mother played to us Beethoven, Schumann, Schubert, Mozart, Chopin, or read aloud to us from Shakespeare, Shelley, Keats, or Burns. Those hours were to us enchanted."

Eager to contribute to the family's always scarce funds, Isadora—still a child herself—began to take baby-sitting jobs. To keep her young charges amused, she conducted a "school of the dance," which consisted largely of instructing the children to wave their arms in the air. As Isadora grew up, she became increasingly interested in "aesthetic dancing," a combination of self-expression and exercise that was just coming into vogue.

In the late 19th century, the puritanical tradition in the United States was still strong. "Nice" women did not reveal their bodies; their clothing concealed them from toe to shoulder. A "nice" woman could dance in a ballroom, but she would never think of dancing as a performer. Americans, however, had always respected the idea of physical fitness; exercise, therefore, was considered both acceptable and desirable.

Workers rest during the excavation of ancient Troy, unearthed by German archaeologist Heinrich Schliemann at Hisarlik, Turkey, in 1871. The passion for Greek culture that swept America during Duncan's childhood was due in large part to Schliemann's discoveries.

Spurred in part by the news that archaeologists had unearthed the lost city of Troy, a tide of interest in ancient Greek art and culture swept the United States in the 1870s and 1880s. Lectures about Greek art were popular, and many American homes boasted prints of Athens's Acropolis or copies of classical Greek statues. Prosperous citizens of a secure and newly powerful nation, Americans saw themselves as the heirs of the highly cultured Athenian democracy that had flourished thousands of years earlier.

One product of the public's fascination with classical art was a fad known as "Greek statue posing," in which women formed tableaus (motionless scenes) of ancient sculptures. Statue posing allowed "nice" women to shed their tight corsets, exercise their imaginations, and still remain perfectly respectable.

A natural sequel was "aesthetic gymnastics," a system of "scientific" body movements developed by a French teacher of music and drama, Francois Delsarte. He asserted that the human body had nine sections, each of which could work harmoniously with the others—as long as people followed his system of moving with, not against, the pull of gravity.

Ultraconservatives denounced Delsartian exercises as indecent and immoral, but a door had been opened. Next came "artistic dancing," spontaneous skipping and twirling to the accompaniment of classical music. More and more women began to take off their shoes and leap and sway with the rhythm.

All these dance innovations excited Isadora, who was suffering through the discipline of school. The only subject she liked was reading; she devoured everything from Shakespeare's plays to romantic "dime novels." Finally, when she was about 13 years old, she decided to quit school for good. Pinning up her hair in a "ladylike" bun, she announced she was

The mansion of railroad tycoon Charles Crocker was one of many ornate residences built in newly prosperous, late-19th-century San Francisco. Duncan often taught dance at such homes.

16 and went into business as a dancing instructor.

At first she worked with her older brothers and sister, who had started teaching "social" dancing, the formal waltzes and polkas that people did at fancy balls. Soon, however, she was holding her own classes, offering instruction in her version of artistic dancing. "I followed my fantasy and improvised, teaching any pretty thing that came into my head," she recalled in her autobiography. She based one of her first dances on the lines, "I shot an arrow into the air/It fell to earth, I knew not where," from "The Song of the Arrow," by Henry Wadsworth Longfellow. "I used to recite the poem," she said later, "and teach the children to follow its meaning in gesture and movement."

Isadora was an unusually graceful young woman. Undoubtedly hoping their daughters would develop similar grace, neighborhood parents eagerly brought their little girls to her dancing classes. Word of her teaching abilities spread, and she soon began to receive invitations to instruct wealthy girls in some of San Francisco's most elegant mansions.

Still, she had little formal training in dance. At the suggestion of a family friend, Isadora's mother enrolled her in ballet school. The most brilliant dancing the Western world had ever produced, ballet had grown immensely popular by the mid-19th century. One reason for its great appeal was the invention of toe shoes—slippers with stiff points, reinforced with wood and glue, that let dancers waft around on the very tips of their toes. These shoes gave ballerinas a new delicacy and grace, which captivated their audiences.

Then, too, there was the glamour of the ballet. Developed in France and Italy, ballet had taken root in Russia by the time Isadora was born. There, supported by the czars (rulers) and their glittering courts, it had become a fantastic, extravagant entertainment. Dances were created with fairy-tale plots—the romantic *Sleeping Beauty*, the tragic *Swan Lake*—and performed in magnificent costumes. The great ballerinas of the age were as well known and admired as movie stars are today.

In a way it was this very splendor that would lead to ballet's decline in Russia. Audiences kept demanding new, more glamorous effects, and dancemasters had to comply, often at the expense of producing interesting dancing. When the great European ballets were performed in the United States, they seemed dazzling, but undeniably "foreign." In those days, America had no real ballet of its own. It had a few famous dancers, but most of the big stars were European.

By the time Isadora was old enough to see a ballet, many of the dances were spectacular to look at, but stiff and predictable. They told their stories through sign language or pantomime (wordless acting) rather than through movement. For example, a dancer might point to her head to mean "the prince," then to her eye to mean "has seen," bringing her hands to her heart to signify "the girl he loves," pointing to the floor to mean "here," and raising her hands over her head to show "this evening."

To Isadora, such movements seemed artificial and dull, and the established techniques of the ballet seemed even worse. She rebelled

Costumed for an 1890 performance, 12-year-old Isadora Duncan displays the poise that would, only a few years later, help to make her a reigning star of the dance world.

Duncan demonstrates the "ladylike" style that made her a popular instructor; many San Francisco parents wanted her to teach their daughters to sit, stand, and walk with similar grace.

against her lessons, just as she had against school. "When the teacher told me to stand on my toes," she recalled, "I asked him why, and when he replied, 'Because it is beautiful,' I said that it was ugly and against nature, and after the third lesson I left his class, never to return."

Later she would refer to ballet's strict system of steps as "stiff and commonplace gymnastics." "I dreamed of a different dance," she wrote. "I was feeling out towards an invisible world into which I divined I might enter if I found the key."

By "an invisible world," she meant human emotion. She wanted to find a kind of dance that could express the human spirit. Nothing would be false; all the motions would be natural, like the movements of an animal or the rippling of water. Because the movements would be natural, she felt, they would be beautiful. Although only 16, she was beginning to lay the groundwork for her art.

Despite his estrangement from his wife and children, Joseph Duncan had remained concerned about their welfare. In 1894, he made a business comeback and bought his family a large house. The new residence included a spacious barn, in which the delighted Duncans began to offer amateur theatricals as well as dancing lessons.

The family shows featured dances by Isadora, poetry recitals by her

Gorgeously dressed dancers of the Russian Imperial Ballet perform choreographer Marius Petipa's A Midsummer Night's Dream *in 1876, the height of Russian ballet's golden age.*

brother Augustin, and short comic plays starring all four children. The productions proved so popular that the Duncans went on the road, presenting them in towns up and down the California coast. This period of prosperity, however, was short-lived. Two years after he bought the family's house, Joseph Duncan went bankrupt once again, and the house was sold. Isadora Duncan decided that the time had come for her to support the family.

Duncan portrays a fairy in Augustin Daly's 1896 production of A Midsummer
Night's Dream. *The costume's paper wings annoyed her; she would have much
preferred imaginary wings.*

TWO

Finding an Audience

Isadora Duncan had already started building a reputation in the theater, and she knew she was destined for a glorious career. At the age of 16, she had wangled an audition with a drama company then performing in San Francisco. As her mother played the piano—Felix Mendelssohn's "Spring Song"—the manager watched in silence. Then, recalled Duncan in her autobiography, he turned to her mother and said, "This sort of thing is no good for a theater. It's more for a church. I advise you to take your little girl home."

But Duncan remained undaunted, confident in her talent. So did her mother, who, Duncan recalled, was always "ready to follow me anywhere." Calling a family council, Isadora announced her plan to head for Chicago, where she would "make the family's fortune." Her sister and brothers would follow her there once she achieved success.

Duncan and her mother arrived in Chicago on a hot day in June 1895. Their possessions included a few pieces of old-fashioned jewelry, a small trunk, and $25. "I expected that I would have an engagement at once, and that everything would be very pleasant and simple," Duncan wrote later.

Carrying the short, white Greek tunic she always wore when performing, the 17-year-old dancer plodded through the streets, seeking auditions. She danced for one manager after another, but each, she recalled, had the same response: "It's very lovely, but *not* for the theater."

Soon the Duncans were reduced to pawning their jewelry. Finally the day came when their landlord locked them out "on the street without a penny." Isadora sold her last possession, an antique lace collar, for $10. She used part of the money to pay for another room. With the rest she bought a large box of tomatoes, the cheapest food she could find. Later she would write that after the summer of 1895, she could never visit Chicago without "a sickening feeling of hunger."

When her mother became so weak she could barely rise from her bed, Duncan applied for work at a local vaudeville theater. Conceding that she was graceful and pretty, the manager said that if she would drop "the Greek thing," and do "something with skirts and frills and kicks," he would hire her for $50 per week.

Desperate, she took the job. Billed as "The California Faun," she danced for a week—and then quit. She had, she said later, "had enough of trying to amuse the public with something which was against my ideals. And that was the first and last time I ever did so."

Now she learned that Augustin Daly, an important New York producer, was in Chicago, and she managed to get an appointment with him. She treated him to a long speech about "the art of the dance." She was offering him, she said, "the idea that is going to revolutionize our entire epoch"; she would bring to his theater "the vital soul that it lacks, the soul of the dancer."

When Daly was able to speak, he said he was preparing to stage a pantomime in New York City, and that he would give her "a little part" in it. "Overcome with delight," Isadora raced home, told her mother the good news, and fired off a telegram to a friend in San Francisco: "TRIUMPHANT ENGAGEMENT. AUGUSTIN DALY. MUST REACH NEW YORK FIRST OCTOBER. WIRE A HUNDRED DOLLARS FOR FARE."

The telegram brought not only the money but Augustin, Raymond, and Elizabeth Duncan. Hearing of their sister's "triumphant engagement," they had concluded that the family's fortunes were made and borrowed money for the train fare. In New York, the Duncans moved into an inexpensive boardinghouse and Isadora reported for work at Daly's theater.

She was far from delighted by her role. "When I was told," she wrote, "that I must press my heart to say LOVE, and then violently hit myself on the chest to say ME, it all seemed to be too ridiculous." Nevertheless, she played her part for three weeks, then went on the road with the show for two months, earning $15 per week. She was happy to get the money, most of which she gave her mother, but she never learned to like pantomime. "If you want to speak, why don't you speak?" she wrote later. "Why all this effort to make gestures as in a deaf and dumb asylum?"

She continued to perform with the

Daly troupe, playing such small parts as that of a dancing fairy in *A Midsummer Night's Dream*. After two years, she decided to resign from the company. She had worked hard, but she felt no closer to her goal: bringing the world a new kind of dancing.

Isadora's sister, Elizabeth, had opened a dancing school in New York, and the Duncans had begun to rent their rooms by the hour to music teachers. The family, however, was still desperately short of money. Isadora looked for ways to help, but the only dancing performed in public was ballet or music-hall entertainment, and her style fit neither category. She did, however, arrange to make occasional appearances at small afternoon recitals. One of the first was a program called "An Afternoon with Omar Khayyám," in which she illustrated verses from the Persian poet's *Rubáiyát*. Attended primarily by wealthy and conservative society matrons, the recital was not an unqualified success.

According to one newspaper report, when Duncan appeared, "Her arms were bare to the shoulder, as were her legs to the knee." Such exposure of the body was genuinely shocking to late 19th-century society. Women's daytime clothing in this period completely covered the legs and upper arms. A ballet dancer's legs could be visible, but only when clothed in tights; even Anna Pavlova, the most celebrated bal-

Swathed in her mother's curtains, Duncan strikes a romantic pose in this 1898 portrait, made by New York society photographer Jacob Schloss. She used this picture on her calling cards.

let star of the era, wore a corset when she danced. Isadora Duncan's "indecent exposure" at the Khayyám performance caused 40 women to stalk out of the recital hall in horror.

Nevertheless, some of the less easily shocked observers were intrigued with Duncan's "revolutionist" art. She began to receive invitations to dance at the palatial estates of such wealthy

Society matrons attend a garden party in Newport, Rhode Island. Duncan often danced at such events, but, she said, she suspected her work was "slightly above the heads" of her "well-fed" audiences.

families as the Astors and the Vanderbilts. To the music of Johann Strauss, Mendelssohn, and other romantic composers, or sometimes to the accompaniment of recited poetry, she presented dances that she called "The Spirit of Spring" or "A Dance of Wandering."

Although Duncan became "a society pet," her wealthy patrons were rarely generous in paying her for her performances. Trips to Newport, Rhode Island, and other fashionable resorts usually netted her barely enough to pay for transportation. Furthermore, although Duncan found the society audiences "affable," none of them, she said, had "the slightest understanding of what I was doing."

Once again restless, she began, she recalled, "to feel a strong wish to find some more congenial atmosphere than New York." She dreamed of London, "and the writers and painters one might meet there—George Meredith, Henry James, [George] Watts, [Algernon] Swinburne, [Edward] Burne-Jones, [James] Whistler."

Duncan once said that she could not understand "why, if one wanted to do a thing, one should not do it. I have never waited to do as I wished." Going to England was no exception; to pay for her family's passage, she appealed to the wealthy women for whom she had been performing. She managed to raise only $300, not enough for regular steamship tickets, but her brother Raymond came up with a "bright idea." He searched, recalled his sister, "around the wharves until he found a small cattle boat going to Hull. The captain of this ship was so touched by Raymond's story that he consented to take us as passengers"—free of charge.

Before their May 1899 voyage to England, the 21-year-old Duncan gave another recital, this one reviewed with even less enthusiasm than the Khayyám performance. Her attire was once again the critics' chief complaint. "Her sole costume for yesterday's dance was a species of surgical bandage of gauze and satin of the hue of raspberry ice," sneered one reviewer. "When the final dance was finished," he continued, "there was a sigh of relief that it was over and that Miss Duncan's bandages hadn't fallen off, as they threatened to do during the entire show."

The critic also reported that "the audience of tortured souls gazed at one another and blushed or giggled" as they watched Duncan's "writhing and painful leaps and hops." He concluded by calling Duncan's plan to go to London "sad, considering we are at peace with England at present."

Never downcast by the views of

Isadora and Raymond Duncan were excited by the British Museum's treasures, especially such Greek antiquities as this marble frieze, which had once adorned a wall of the Parthenon.

those who "had no art sense whatever," the four Duncans (Augustin had married and remained in the United States) set off for England in high spirits. In her autobiography, Duncan said that except for the "bellowings and moanings of the poor cattle in the hold," the trip was "a very happy time," filled with "irrepressible merriment and delight."

In London, said Duncan, she felt like "a fish that has found the water to which it belongs." She and her family spent their days on buses, driving through the city "in a state of perfect ecstasy, and in amazement and delight of everything around us." Their favorite spot was the British Museum, where

Isadora and her brother spent hours each day.

Already fascinated with ancient Greece and its ideals of beauty, they joyfully immersed themselves in a study of the museum's vast collection of Greek sculpture and painted vases. Many showed dancers in motion; Isadora imitated their positions, trying to catch the rhythms of the long-silent music. As a mature artist, her work would reflect a number of influences, including Renaissance art, ballet, primitive dancing, and Delsartian movement, but its starting point was the culture of Greece.

The Duncans adored London, but they were faced with their usual prob-lem: a lack of money. After a few months, Elizabeth returned to New York, planning to reopen her dancing school. She would share its income with Isadora, Raymond, and Dora Duncan, none of whom could bear the thought of going home. Meanwhile, Isadora had a stroke of good luck.

Dancing by themselves in a London park one day, she and Raymond were observed by Mrs. Patrick Campbell, one of England's most celebrated actresses. Duncan described the ensuing scene in her autobiography: "Where on earth did you people come from?" asked Campbell. "Not from earth at all," answered Isadora, "but from the moon." "Well," responded the actress,

Nineteenth-century Londoners cruise sedately through Hyde Park. Isadora and Raymond Duncan considered the city's vast, leafy parks perfect settings for spur-of-the-moment dancing.

"whether from the earth or the moon, you are very sweet. Won't you come and see me?"

Quickly accepting, the Duncans followed their new friend home, where Isadora delighted Campbell with her dancing. Intrigued, the actress introduced the young Americans to her circle of wealthy friends. Isadora was soon performing in the drawing rooms of London's cultural and social elite. The passion for everything Greek had swept the city, making Duncan's Greek-inspired costumes and movements particularly popular.

One of her admirers was Charles Hallé, a well-known painter whose interest in her would be important in her development as an artist. Hallé, director of a prestigious gallery that specialized in modern art, invited Duncan to give a series of recitals there. In the spring and early summer of 1900, London's "smart set" flocked to Hallé's Regent Street gallery, where Duncan presented three "Evenings."

The day after her first performance, the London *Times* carried a review by J. Fuller-Maitland, a distinguished musical authority. He described her as "a young dancer of remarkable skill whose art, though it may fail to satisfy the average ballet master, has wonderful eloquence of its own." Another critic wrote, "She dances Mendelssohn's musical poem, 'A Welcome to Spring,' with frolicsome, laughing

Actress Mrs. Patrick Campbell, seen here in a London production of The Foolish Virgin, *was charmed by Duncan, whom she first saw dancing in a public park.*

grace that makes one think of flowers and birds and lambs at play.... The whole dance seems like something that might have happened in ancient Greece."

On Duncan's first "Evening," her dancing was accompanied by spoken poetry. Visiting her after the show, Fuller-Maitland suggested that she try

Duncan (center), who said London made her feel like "a fish that has found the water to which it belongs," attends an art exhibition in the British capital in 1900.

she began to concentrate instead on the *rhythm* of the music to which she danced.

Duncan's style was beginning to evolve and her reputation was growing. To make a living, however, she needed theatrical bookings, and British theater managers showed no interest in her work. Impatient with his sister's slow progress toward success, Raymond Duncan left London for Paris in the late spring of 1900. "He bombarded us with telegrams imploring us to come to Paris," recalled Duncan, "so one day Mother and I packed up our belongings and took the [English] Channel boat."

Just as the Duncans had excitedly toured London, they now prowled the streets of Paris, gazing with awe at the city's gardens, sculptures, churches, and museums. Here it was the Louvre, Paris's great art museum, that Isadora and Raymond Duncan haunted. "The Louvre was our paradise," wrote Isadora Duncan. "We spent so much time in the Greek vase room that the guardian grew suspicious and when I explained in pantomime [she did not yet speak French] that I had only come there to dance, he decided that he had to do with harmless lunatics, so he let us alone."

Several months after the Duncans' Paris reunion, Charles Hallé arrived to visit the *Exposition Universelle*, the largest world's fair ever held up to that

dancing to the waltzes of the 19th-century Polish composer, Frédéric Chopin. She followed his advice, whirling to Chopin's expressive, romantic melodies during her next two performances. This was an important development in Duncan's career. Until now, she had designed her dances as illustrations of poems or well-known stories. After listening to Fuller-Maitland, time. He escorted Isadora Duncan to the fair, where, for the first time, she saw the towering work of the great French sculptor Auguste Rodin. Studying Rodin's statues, which treat the human body as the outward expression of the human soul, Duncan felt that she was in the presence of a kindred spirit.

She and Hallé also attended many performances at the small theater where Loie Fuller danced. Fuller, an extraordinary American dancer who had taken Paris by storm, was to have a strong influence on her young countrywoman.

When Hallé returned to London, his wealthy Parisian friends continued to invite Duncan to their homes. Once again she found herself dancing in elegant drawing rooms, once again praised by the community's wealthiest and most cultured people. After her performances, the Parisians would applaud and cheer: *"Bravo, bravo, comme elle est exquise!"* (How exquisite she is) and *"Quelle jolie enfant!"* (What a pretty child).

Once she had acquired a following in Paris, Duncan began to hold recitals for paying patrons in the one-room studio she shared with her mother and brother. Parisians were amused by her novel invitations to these performances. One of them, dated December 12, 1901, reads: "Miss Duncan will dance to the sound of harp and flute in

Auguste Rodin, whose famous sculptures include The Thinker *and* The Kiss, *stands before one of his works in Paris. A great admirer of Duncan's dancing, Rodin made several drawings of her.*

her studio next Thursday evening and, if you feel that seeing this small person dancing against the waves of an overpowering destiny is of ten francs' benefit to you—why come along!"

Duncan devoted her days in Paris to refining her theory of dance. She spent hours at the library of the Paris Opéra,

The Opéra was one of the Parisian monuments adored by Isadora Duncan and her family. "Our young American souls," she wrote, were "uplifted before this culture, which we had striven so hard to find."

where, as she put it, "I applied myself to the task of reading everything that had ever been written on the art of dancing, from the earliest Egyptians to the present day." She also worked hard at her studio, testing the principles of the new dance she believed she could offer the world.

Conventional ballet defines the base of the spine as the center, or axis, of movement. But Duncan decided that this "spring of all movement" was lo-cated in the center of the chest. In dancing, she moved forward with the upper part of her body first; from there, she believed, motion unfolded outward to all other parts of the body. Another difference between ballet and Duncan's emerging style involved the force of gravity. Leaping and spinning in midair, a ballet dancer gives the illusion of flight, of defying the earth's pull. Duncan, on the other hand, *used* the floor, stepping and springing on it in a variety of ways, sometimes kneeling, and even lying, as though to emphasize the body's weight.

Her dancing appeared to be spontaneous—made up as she went along—but its simplicity was deceptive. In fact, Duncan composed her dances very carefully, plotting out the movements and rehearsing them well. Duncan, who had gone from ballet slippers to sandals, now began to dance barefoot. This unheard-of practice was to become a kind of trademark for her, used both by those who scorned her as a "barefoot dancer" and by her admirers. Whenever she could arrange it, she had a carpet, which provided traction, placed on the stage. She also began performing in front of simple draperies, so that her audience would concentrate on the dance, not on the scenery. The blue-gray curtains that she later took with her on tours became another Duncan trademark.

She was in the midst of all these experiments when, late in 1901, a surprise visitor appeared at her studio. It was Loie Fuller, the celebrated American dancer whose revolutionary theatrics had thrilled Duncan and Hallé at the Paris Exposition. The toast of avant-garde (culturally advanced) Paris, Fuller had been painted by Henri Toulouse-Lautrec, sculpted by Rodin, and honored by authors and composers. Her presence was eagerly sought by members of the city's high society.

Nike of Samothrace, the celebrated 4th-century B.C. marble statue popularly known as Winged Victory, was among the sights that awed Duncan when she visited the Louvre, Paris's great art museum.

Born in Illinois in 1862, Fuller had created a sensation in Paris with her 1892 "Fire Dance," in which she

Portraying a butterfly, American dancer Loie Fuller swirls across the stage in a cloud of glowing fabric. Like most Paris theatergoers, Duncan was dazzled by Fuller, whom she called a "genius."

danced on a pane of glass suspended above flamelike lights. She left a permanent mark on theatrical history, particularly with her experiments in stage lighting. Unlike conventional dancers, she performed in a totally darkened theater, its stage dramatically illuminated by an extraordinary combination of revolving lights, mirrors, colored gelatins, and magic-lantern projectors that showed elaborately painted slides. Her costumes—clouds of glistening, filmy cloth—were accentuated by a stark backdrop of black velvet.

"Before our very eyes," reported Duncan, "she turned into many-colored, shining orchids, to a wavering, flowering sea flower, and at length to a spiral-like lily, all the magic of Merlin, the sorcery of light, color, flowing form. . . . No imitator of Loie Fuller has ever been able even to hint at her genius!"

Now this spectacular creature was standing at the entrance of Duncan's little studio. "Naturally I danced for her," recalled Duncan. She also treated Fuller to an elaborate explanation of her theories on the dance. Fuller, who was leaving for a concert tour in Germany the following day, was clearly

The Eiffel Tower, the world's tallest structure when it was built in 1889, rises 984 feet above the Paris exposition of 1900. The fair attracted 47 million people, including Isadora Duncan.

impressed; she invited Duncan to join her on the trip to Germany. "I was only too delighted to accept," recalled Duncan. The next morning, she was on her way to Berlin.

А. ДУНКАНЪ.

1020.

Duncan personifies "new woman," one of her favorite themes. The woman of the future, she said, would be a "free spirit," representing "the highest intelligence in the freest body."

THREE

Conquering Europe

By the time she was 23, Isadora Duncan had seen far more of the world than many American women twice her age. Sophisticated and self-assured, she was nevertheless unprepared for some of the people and situations she encountered when she left Paris in 1901.

First of all, there was Loie Fuller herself. Duncan's early admiration for the colorful dancer's work grew even stronger when she saw her perform in Germany. After Fuller's first Berlin show, Duncan recalled, she "returned to the hotel dazzled and carried away by this marvelous artist." And she was stunned by the "magnificent" hotel suites and "extravagant" meals she found herself sharing with the Fuller entourage.

From Berlin, the Fuller troupe traveled to Leipzig and Munich, and then to Vienna, Austria, where Duncan was joined by her mother. There, to Duncan's delight, Fuller arranged a solo recital for her. The audience included most of the city's artistic community, along with a sprinkling of diplomats and society people. It also included Alexander Gross, an impresario (producer) from Budapest, Hungary. After Duncan's performance, Gross went backstage. "When you wish to find a future," he told the dancer, "seek me in Budapest."

At first Duncan declined Gross's offer, which was a contract for a series of solo recitals in the Hungarian capital's most important theater. "My dancing is for the elite, for the artists, sculptors, painters, musicians," she told Gross, "but not for the general public." Gross, however, assured her that if artists liked her dancing, the public would like it "a hundred times more." Finally, in April 1902, Duncan and her mother left for Budapest. It was one of the most important moves she had ever made.

Never hampered by self-consciousness in dancing or in speech, Duncan described her Budapest opening as "an indescribable triumph." She was indeed received with an outpouring of enthusiasm. "She has discovered entirely new movements of the human body," observed one newspaper critic the day after her first performance. Another credited her with the ability "to impart something that we feel we have seen once in a dream."

Duncan gave 30 standing-room-only performances, each followed by clamorous demands for encores. Deciding to try something new one night, she asked the orchestra to play Austrian composer Johann Strauss's 1867 waltz, "The Blue Danube," named for the river that flows through the center of Budapest. Improvising as she danced, she gave an impassioned interpretation of the popular melody. "The effect," she said later, "was an electric shock. The whole audience sprang to their feet in such a delirium of enthusiasm that I had to repeat the waltz many times before they would behave less like mad people."

At this performance was one special fan. He was Oscar Beregi, an actor whom Duncan later romantically de-

Hungarian actor Oscar Beregi, Duncan's first great love, plays a scene with actress Norma Talmadge in the 1927 film Camille. *Duncan was emotionally shattered when her romance with Beregi ended in 1902.*

scribed as "a young Hungarian of god-like features and stature." Duncan was young and beautiful; Beregi was young and handsome. It was spring. Not surprisingly, the two fell in love. For weeks, Duncan was so absorbed in her new relationship that she could think of little else. Nevertheless, both lovers continued to work; Duncan danced, and Beregi played Romeo in the Hungarian version of Shakespeare's *Romeo and Juliet*.

Duncan and Beregi "swore fidelity till death," but problems arose after only a few weeks. Dora Duncan was "anguished" over her daughter's behavior (in the highly moral Victorian era, one simply did not conduct an open love affair), and Elizabeth Duncan, who had just arrived from New York, "seemed to think," Duncan wrote later, "that I had committed some crime."

Beregi assumed that he and Duncan would marry, and that she would automatically give up her career to help him with his. She was now faced with a painful question: Did gaining love mean losing art? She felt compelled to pursue her own vision of dance—she had just enjoyed her first taste of public acclaim—yet she also yearned to devote herself to those she loved. These two desires were, and would continue to be, in direct conflict throughout her life.

When Beregi realized that Duncan would not abandon her ambitions, he suggested that they go their separate ways. Duncan was crushed. "I still remember," she wrote many years later, "the cold chill that struck my breast" at Beregi's words. Emotionally shattered, she was in no condition to dance, so Gross and his wife took her to a German resort to recover. Here she

Duncan performs in Munich, Germany, in 1902. Resented at first by the city's artistic community, she became wildly popular, especially with local students, who mobbed her wherever she went.

spent several weeks, "languid and sad," as she put it in her autobiography, "refusing to be interested either in the beautiful country or the kind friends about me."

She finally became aware that she had spent most of the money she had earned in Budapest; she could afford to be "languid and sad" no longer. "I remember bursting into tears," she wrote later, "and swearing never to desert art for love again." Although she would try, this was not an oath that Isadora Duncan would be able to keep.

Once Duncan recovered, the pace of her career began to quicken. In November 1902 she rejoined her mother and sister in Munich, Germany, where Gross had booked a concert for her at the Künstler Haus (artists' house). At first, many of the artists and writers who made Künstler Haus their headquarters opposed Duncan's appearance there. Her dancing, they said, would be a "sacrilege" to their "temple of art."

Hoping to convert some of these critics, Duncan paid a call on one of their most prominent spokesmen, painter and sculptor Franz von Stuck. She made her point in typical Duncan fashion: "I took off my dress in his studio," she recalled later, "donned my tunic, and danced for him, then talked to him for four hours without stopping, on the holiness of my mission and the possibility of the dance as an art."

Von Stuck, according to Duncan, later told friends that he had never been so "astonished" in his life—that he "felt as if a dryad [wood nymph] from Mount Olympus had suddenly appeared." Duncan's mission was a success. "Of course," she wrote, "he

gave his consent, and my debut at the Munich Künstler Haus was the greatest artistic event and sensation that the town had experienced in many years."

Although most of her critics changed their minds when they saw Duncan dance, a few continued to deride her unconventional performance style. German newspapers began to run frequent articles about Duncan, some praising her and others ridiculing her. The controversy, which gave Duncan's career a strong push, delighted Alexander Gross. News of the impassioned debate even reached the United States: "Isadora Duncan's Poetic Dances Have Divided Germany," headlined one St. Louis newspaper story.

Duncan's uninhibited offstage activities did nothing to quiet the furor raised by her dancing. The new idol of Munich's student population, she was often escorted through the streets by young men carrying lighted torches and bellowing student songs. "One night they bore me off to their student cafe, where they lifted me dancing from one table to another. All night they sang," she reported in her autobiography.

Munich's more straitlaced citizens were shocked by such behavior, but Duncan insisted that it was all "most innocent"—in spite of the fact "that even my dress and shawl were torn to ribbons and worn in their caps when they carried me home at dawn."

Gross, a master impresario, now arranged for Duncan's debut in Berlin. This was the performance, staged in March 1903 at the enormous Kroll Opera House, that had been so eagerly awaited by the cultural elite of the German capital—the triumphant appearance that made "the Divine Isadora" a familiar phrase. From this point on, most of the world ignored her last name; she was known to people everywhere simply as "Isadora."

The Berlin Opera House was rocked with shouts, cheers, and applause when Isadora Duncan completed her two-hour performance. After demanding and receiving many encores, the audience rushed to the front of the theater. "Hundreds of young students actually climbed upon the stage," reported Duncan, "until I was in danger of being crushed to death by too much adoration."

One of the pieces that had produced such excitement among the Berlin audience was Duncan's "Dance of the Future," which she had based on the famous 15th-century painting, *Primavera (Spring)*. The work of Italian artist Sandro Botticelli, *Primavera* shows a female figure, dressed in flowing robes and surrounded by gracefully swaying dancers on a field of flowers.

"Inspired by this picture," recalled Duncan in her autobiography, "I cre-

Sculptor Walter Schott, one of the many artists to use Duncan as a model, stands before his statue of the dancer in 1903, with Dora (left) and Isadora Duncan.

ated a dance in which I endeavored to realize the soft and marvelous movements emanating from it; the soft undulation of the flower-covered earth, the circle of nymphs and the flight of the zephyrs, all assembling about the central figure, half Aphrodite [the ancient Greek goddess of love and beauty], half Madonna [the Virgin Mary], who indicates the procreation [birth] of spring in one significant gesture."

Sandro Botticelli's 15th-century masterpiece, Primavera (Spring), *inspired Duncan to create one of her most famous works, the* Dance of the Future *(left).*

The "Dance of the Future" was pure Duncan. With it, she said, "I may show others the way to richness of life and development of joy." After the concert, she was showered with the richness of Berlin; the city seemed to throw itself at her feet. Artists painted and sculpted her; newspaper cartoonists, some admiring and some malicious, caricatured her; wealthy hostesses gave lavish parties in her honor. Isadora Duncan was famous.

In April 1903 she gave a lecture on the dance at the Berlin Press Club. Her speech, widely quoted in newspapers around the world, predicted that "woman's body" would soon "return to the original strength and to natural movements," leading to "the development of perfect mothers and the birth of healthy and beautiful children."

Duncan's lecture emphasized her conviction that dance is not mere entertainment, but an art based on nature. "Oh, she is coming," proclaimed Duncan, "the dancer of the future: the free spirit who will inhabit the body of new woman . . . the highest intelligence in the freest body!"

Now Duncan toured Paris and the cities of Germany, creating a sensation at every stop. As her fame grew, her income soared; for the first time in her life, she felt "rich." In the early summer of 1903, Augustin and Raymond Duncan joined their mother and two sisters in Munich. With their newly hefty bank balance, the reunited "Clan Duncan" decided to realize a long-cherished dream—"of making a pilgrimage," wrote Isadora Duncan, "to the very holiest shrine of art, of going to our beloved Athens."

Alexander Gross pleaded with his star client not to interrupt her fast-advancing career, but Isadora Duncan and her family were determined to see Greece, the land they considered the source of all art and beauty. In charge of the trip was Raymond, the family member most steeped in Greek history and legend. He decreed that their journey would be "as primitive as possible," recreating the travels of Ulysses in Homer's epic poem, the *Odyssey*.

When the Duncans arrived on the Greek coast, Raymond chartered a small fishing boat in which the family headed across the Ionian Sea to the village of Karvassaras. On board was the food Raymond considered appropriate: goat cheese, black olives, and dried fish. "I shall never forget, to my dying day," recalled Isadora Duncan wryly, "the smell of that cheese and fish, exposed all day to a blazing sun, especially as the little boat had a gentle but potent rolling gait of its own."

Putting ashore at Karvassaras, Isadora and Raymond Duncan knelt down to kiss the ground. "Indeed," recalled Duncan, "we were half mad with joy. We wanted to embrace all the inhabitants of the village and cry, 'At last we have arrived, after many wanderings, in the sacred land of Hellas [the ancient Greek name for Greece]!' "

Next, making their way by foot, horse and carriage, boat, and train, the family went to Athens. Deeply moved by the sights along the way, they often threw their arms around each other and wept. "The stolid peasants," remembered Isadora Duncan, "eyed us with wonder. They probably thought we were either drunk or crazy."

Finally, the Duncans reached Athens, the capital of Greece. When they saw the ruins of the Parthenon, the ancient temple of the goddess Athena, they felt, recalled Isadora Duncan, that they "had reached the pinnacle of perfection." They asked themselves, she added, "why we should ever leave Greece, since we found in Athens everything which satisfied our esthetic sense."

To the emotional family, the answer was obvious. "We decided," recalled the dancer, "that the Clan Duncan should remain in Athens eternally, and there build a temple that should be characteristic of us." The site of the temple would be a tract of land Duncan bought two miles east of Athens.

As a first step toward their new life, they discarded all their modern clothes. Although they had long worn Grecian robes for dancing and special occasions, now they dressed exclusively in tunics and sandals—drawing some questioning glances from the 20th-century Greeks around them.

Then, aglow with enthusiasm, they made rules for their new life-style: None of them would marry (except Augustin, who was already married). Each morning, they would "greet the rising sun with joyous songs and dances." Sunrise would be followed by consumption of "a modest bowl of goat's milk" (they would become vegetarians) and "teaching the inhabitants to dance and sing." Afternoons "were to be spent in meditation, and the evenings given over to pagan ceremonies with appropriate music."

The Duncans did their best, but the path to their goal was strewn with difficulties. For one thing, there was no water anywhere near their land, something they had failed to notice when they bought it. For another, the tract was on a remote hillside; hauling the huge stones required for their temple proved difficult, time-consuming, and very expensive.

Practicality about finances was never among the Duncan family's traits. The temple was far from completion when, after a year, Isadora Duncan realized she had almost run out of money. She also came to a conclusion: "We were not, nor ever could be, other than moderns. We could not have the feelings of the ancient Greeks." Furthermore, she reasoned, her family was "Scotch-Irish-American," and perhaps

The Parthenon, which still stands in Athens, enchanted the Duncans when they saw it in 1903. Completed in 438 B.C., the magnificent marble temple was dedicated to Athena, the virgin goddess of wisdom.

Overjoyed to be in Athens, Duncan dances in an ancient temple. This photograph was taken by the dancer's brother Raymond, who had organized the family's 1903 expedition to Greece.

"nearer allied to the Red Indian than to the Greeks." As impulsively as they had decided to go to Greece, the Duncans decided to leave it. Abandoning their hillside and its piles of expensive rocks, they boarded a train for Vienna.

There Duncan resumed her schedule of concert tours. Now she included in her performance a new dance based on ancient Greek themes, along with a speech about the place of dance in Greek tragedy. Duncan's Austrian and German fans were not enthusiastic about her new material; audience members often shouted such suggestions as "Forget the Greeks—dance 'The Blue Danube'!"

In the spring of 1904, Duncan received an important visitor. She was Cosima Wagner, daughter of composer Franz Liszt and widow of composer Richard Wagner, whose many operas include *Tannhäuser*, *Lohengrin*, and *Tristan und Isolde*. Cosima Wagner was in charge of the Bayreuth Festival, Europe's most important musical event. Staged each summer since 1876 in the German town of Bayreuth, the festival was entirely dedicated to production of Wagner's operas. (Suspended during World War II, the Bayreuth Festival was reopened by Wagner's grandsons

The Duncan family temple, built on a hill overlooking Athens, was planned as a massive, many-chambered structure. Construction, however, proved extremely costly; the temple was never completed.

in 1951; it continues to draw an international audience of music lovers every year.)

Would Duncan be interested, asked Wagner, in dancing in the coming summer's production of *Tannhäuser*? The Berlin Ballet had already been engaged to dance in the opera, but Wagner felt that Duncan's unique style was closer to her late husband's vision. Duncan was highly flattered by the invitation, but she was hesitant about accepting it.

"With my ideals," she wrote later, "it was impossible for me to have anything to do with the ballet, whose every movement shocked my sense of beauty, and whose expression seemed to me mechanical and vulgar." Nevertheless, she, too, believed that she could deliver a proper interpretation of Wagner's concept.

"I will come," she told Cosima Wagner, "and I will try to give at least an indication of the lovely, soft, voluptuous movements which I already see for the Three Graces." (The Graces, characters in *Tannhäuser*, represent peace and love. According to Wagner's own notes, they embody "the calm, the languor of satisfied amorous sensibility.")

Isadora Duncan arrived in Bayreuth in May 1904. As she did wherever she went, she created a sensation. Ever since her year in Greece she had dressed only in a short, white tunic, her legs bare, her feet encased in sandals—"a most extraordinary sight," one festival staff member observed. Duncan's unconventional offstage activities also stirred up gossip.

The festival was one of Europe's greatest social events; here the wealthy and famous, the royal and the artistic, came to see and be seen. Among the heads of state who attended was King Ferdinand I of Bulgaria. When he called on Cosima Wagner, everyone in the room rose respectfully—except Isadora Duncan. "I was fiercely democratic," she recalled, "and remained gracefully reclining on a couch." Far from annoyed, the king approached Duncan, who soon engaged him in a lively conversation about Greek history. He became a frequent visitor at her residence. The two, as she later put it, "most innocently sat and discoursed on art," but the visits "caused a hullabaloo in Bayreuth, because they took place at midnight." In fact, said Duncan—accurately—"I could not do anything without seeming extravagantly different from other people, and therefore shocking."

When *Tannhäuser* opened, Duncan's clothes were once more the subject of scandalized whispers. "My transparent tunic, showing every part of my dancing body," she recalled, "created some stir amidst the pink-covered legs of the ballet." Cosima Wagner sent Duncan a long white dress, which she begged the dancer to wear under her filmy costume. Duncan refused. "I would dress and dance exactly my way," she said, "or not at all."

Duncan's insistence on doing things "her way" was a mainspring of her character. Although the issue of clothing was by no means the only one on which she disagreed with the society of her time, it cropped up again and again. "Many times I declaimed myself hoarse on the subject . . . of how beautiful and innocent the naked body was when inspired by beautiful thoughts," she remarked later. "I was," she added, "a perfect pagan to all."

For the *Tannhäuser* dance sequence, the stage was filled with traditionally costumed, formally trained ballet dancers; at their center whirled the barefoot Duncan, her unbound hair flying, her white tunic flowing. "Intoxicated" by the music, she said her

Cosima Wagner greets a visitor at Bayreuth, site of the annual German music festival honoring her husband, composer Richard Wagner, who died in 1883. Duncan danced at Bayreuth in the summer of 1904.

"being was vibrating with the waves of Wagner's melody." Her performance was lavishly praised by both audience and critics, several of whom termed it "delightful." As a whole, however, the production was not a success, marred by the jarring blend of two diametrically opposed styles of dance.

It was the first and last time Duncan appeared in a regular ballet. She decided that when she next shared a stage, it would be with dancers she herself had trained. She had, she wrote later, always "conceived the dance as a chorus or community expression." Now she began to think seriously about a school, a place where she could "create an orchestra of dancers."

Isadora Duncan oversees her pupils at the dance school she opened in Berlin in 1904. The school's purpose, she announced, was "to rediscover the beautiful rhythmic movements of the human body."

FOUR

Bold Enterprises

After the summer in Bayreuth, Duncan joined her mother and sister in Berlin. (Augustin had returned to his wife in the United States, and Raymond had gone back to Greece, doggedly continuing to work on the family temple.) Isadora Duncan's thoughts were now concentrated on her dance school. With Dora and Elizabeth Duncan, who shared her enthusiasm for the project, she set out to look for a suitable building.

"With such speediness as marked everything else we did," recalled the dancer, "we found a villa ... and we bought it." The Duncan women went to work furnishing and decorating the suburban "villa," a three-story, yellow house with a large garden. Deciding that the building could accommodate 40 little girls, they bought 40 small beds and covered each with a satin spread. Over every bed, they placed a picture of an angel playing a musical instrument.

Isadora Duncan had elaborate plans for her school, but its opening was delayed by two major events in her life. The first was meeting Gordon Craig.

The son of Ellen Terry, a celebrated British actress whom Duncan had long idolized, Edward Gordon Craig had grown up among theatrical people. He began his own stage career as an actor but soon focused his impressive talents on production, direction, and design. Accused by some of being an impractical visionary, he was hailed by others as one of the most brilliant theatrical craftsmen of modern times.

When Craig began working in the theater, stage designers tried to make their sets look as much like the real world as possible. To the young En-

Gordon Craig and Isadora Duncan enjoy a rare moment of tranquillity in Berlin in 1904. The relationship of the two, who fell in love at first sight, was marked by frequent battles.

strongly influenced other theatrical pioneers of his time and have left an enduring mark on modern stagecraft.

Craig, then 32, first saw the 26-year-old Duncan at the home of mutual friends in 1904. Dressed in her usual tunic and sandals, her dark hair curling around her face, she was listening intently as a fellow guest played the piano. Craig walked across the room to join her. "We became friends and lovers from the moment we stood there at the piano," he later wrote.

The two immediately began to talk of their art, Duncan expounding on "the living, flowing human body," Craig explaining his ideas about "the movement of light, color, and form." Here was a man who spoke Duncan's language; she invited him to come and see her dance.

In his journal (published in 1957), Craig wrote an evocative description of Duncan's performance. "I shall never forget the first time I saw her come on to an empty platform to dance," he wrote. "She came through some small curtains which were not much taller than she herself . . . and in some five or six steps was standing by the piano, quite still."

As her accompanist played the music of Chopin, continued Craig, Duncan took "one step back or sideways, and the music began again as she went moving on before or after it. Only just moving—not pirouetting [spinning on

glishman, this was absurd; he believed that the mission of the theater was to interpret life, not to copy it. Drama, he thought, should stimulate the imagination, offering playgoers *fresh* insights on reality.

So in his own designs, Craig searched for what he called "a magnificent overpowering unity of expression." He envisioned huge, abstract stage settings "on which figures of a heroic mould shall move. . . . All shall be illuminated by a light such as the spheres give us, not such as the footlights give us, but such as we dream of." His imaginative productions one foot] or doing any of those things which we expect to see.... She was speaking in her own language, not echoing any ballet master, and so she came to move as no one had ever seen anyone move before."

Craig found Duncan fascinating. "She was," he said, "telling to the air the very things we longed to hear and till she came we had never dreamed we should hear; and now we heard them, and this sent us all into an unusual state of joy, and I—I sat still and was speechless."

On her part, Duncan was "hypnotized" by the tall and handsome Craig, whom she called "one of the most extraordinary geniuses of our epoch— a creature like [poet Percy Bysshe] Shelley, made of fire and lightning." Instantly and deeply in love, for a time the two thought of nothing but each other. "Here, at last," Duncan wrote later, "was my mate; my love; my self— for we were not two, but one . . . two halves of the same soul."

A powerful intellectual, physical, and emotional bond developed between Duncan and Craig, but each was an iron-willed individualist, so they fought constantly. "After the first two weeks of wild, impassioned lovemaking," recalled Duncan in her autobiography, "there began the waging of the fiercest battle that was ever known, between the genius of Gordon Craig and the inspiration of my art."

Dame Ellen Terry, Gordon Craig's mother, had made a deep impression on Isadora Duncan, who saw her perform in London. The dancer called the actress "my most perfect ideal of woman."

The two baffled each other. Craig wrote that in spite of his "irresistible attraction" to Duncan, he could not decide whether she was "a witch or a pretty child." Duncan was faced with a familiar conflict. "It was my fate," she wrote, "to reconcile the continuing of my career with his love. Impossible combination!"

The second event to delay the opening of Duncan's school came in early 1905, when her manager, Alexander Gross, booked her for a series of concerts in St. Petersburg, Russia. Duncan was reluctant to part from Craig even

Gordon Craig, seen here in a photograph taken by Duncan, was bowled over by the American dancer. "This is a marvelous being," he wrote of her to a friend, "beauty, nature, and brain."

for a few weeks, but a visit to St. Petersburg, the glittering capital of czarist Russia, was too exciting to turn down.

St. Petersburg was also the capital of the ballet world. Paris had long been ballet's main showcase, but in the closing decades of the 19th century, fashionable Parisians had forsaken the Opéra and its sedate dance program. They flocked instead to cabarets and music halls where they could watch gaudily costumed dancers perform the rowdy, high-kicking cancan. Vital, innovative dance had all but disappeared from Paris—but it had reappeared in the east, in the Russian Imperial Ballet. By the time Duncan arrived in St. Petersburg, Russian ballet was in the midst of a golden age.

A major contributor to the magnificence of the Russian ballet was Pyotr Tchaikovsky, composer for such masterpieces as *Swan Lake*, *Sleeping Beauty*, and *The Nutcracker*. Another leading light was Marius Petipa, a French ballet master whose lush, romantic productions earned him the informal title, "master of the grand spectacle."

Among the brilliant dancers performing in Russian ballet at the time of Duncan's first visit to St. Petersburg were the legendary Anna Pavlova and Vaslav Nijinsky, as well as Mathylda Kschessinska, Tamara Karsavina, and Adolph Bolm. The great impresario Sergey Diaghilev, who would later organize the celebrated dance company known as the *Ballets Russes*, was active in Russia, as were *Art Nouveau* painter Léon Bakst and innovative young choreographers Michel Fokine and Léonide Massine.

In full flower at the turn of the century, Russian ballet was about to undergo a rebirth; under the leadership of Diaghilev and Fokine, it would enter the 20th century in an explo-

An immense plaster elephant looms over dancers at an outdoor Paris cabaret. By the late 19th century, French audiences had come to prefer such spectacles to classical ballet.

sively revitalized form. The extravagant spectacle that had characterized late 19th-century classical ballet would give way to a new kind of dance theater, in which music, art, and story would become as essential as the dance itself.

Duncan arrived in Russia the day after Bloody Sunday, a violent incident that foreshadowed the Russian Revolution of 1917. On January 22, 1905, a procession of workers had marched through the streets of St. Petersburg, headed for the palace of Czar Nicholas II with a petition of grievances. The czar's army had greeted the unarmed marchers with a hail of gunfire, killing hundreds.

As Duncan entered St. Petersburg on a bitterly cold January dawn, her carriage met a long, silent line of people carrying row after row of coffins. Duncan was shocked and deeply moved by the sight. "If I had never seen it," she wrote in her autobiography, "all my life would have been different. There, before this seemingly endless procession, this tragedy, I vowed myself and my forces to the service of the people and the downtrodden."

Soldiers patrol a St. Petersburg street after Bloody Sunday, the 1905 massacre in which czarist troops massacred hundreds of Russian workers. The violent incident occurred the day before Duncan's arrival.

Her next view of Russian life was a total contrast. She was lodged in an immense suite at the luxurious Hotel Europa, its rooms filled with exotic flowers, French bonbons, and stacks of invitations from St. Petersburg's elite. Ready for change, their curiosity piqued by reports of Duncan's unconventional ways, the city's aristocratic and artistic leaders had been awaiting her visit with excitement. Her opening-night performance was attended by a huge crowd that included, she later wrote, "the most beautiful women in the world, in marvelous décolleté [low-cut] gowns, covered with jewels, escorted by men in distinguished uniforms."

Duncan wondered how Russians, used to "the gorgeous ballet with its lavish decorations and scenery," would feel as they watched "a young girl, clothed in a tunic of cobweb, appear and dance before a simple blue curtain to the music of Chopin." Her question was answered by the "storm of applause" that followed her first dance.

"There was so much pleasure, such passionate melancholy, such expectation and rapture," wrote one critic later. "Her body is as though bewitched by the music," wrote another. "There is so much sculpture in her, so much color and simplicity, that she fully deserves the capacity audience."

The day after her St. Petersburg debut, Duncan was invited to a performance of the Imperial Ballet by one of its stars, Mathylda Kschessinska. At the theater, the American visitor was seated in a private box and surrounded by "beautiful specimens of the *jeunesse dorée* [gilded youth, or stylish young people] of St. Petersburg." She was, she later recalled, "still wearing my little white tunic and sandals, and must have looked very odd in the midst of this gathering of all the wealth and aristocracy."

Almost against her will, Duncan was impressed with the dancing of Kschessinska. "I am an enemy of the ballet, which I consider a false and preposterous art," she wrote later, "but it was impossible not to applaud the fairy-like figure of [Kschessinska] as she flitted across the stage, more like a lovely bird or butterfly than a human being."

Duncan also admired ballerina Anna Pavlova, "an exquisite apparition" who "floated over the stage." Invited to Pavlova's home to see her work with Marius Petipa, Duncan was amazed by the punishing routines imposed by the ballet master on the fragile-looking young dancer. "The whole tendency of this training," she wrote disapprovingly, "seems to be to separate the gymnastic movements of the body completely from the mind.... This is just the opposite from all the theories on which I founded my school, by which the body becomes transparent and is a medium for the mind and the spirit."

Duncan appreciated the beauty of ballet when it was well performed, but she remained opposed to it on principle. The Russian dancers, on the other hand, not only respected Duncan's work, they sometimes imitated it. Pavlova said the fluid arm movements she used in *The Dying Swan*, one of her greatest roles, were inspired by Duncan. The American dancer, said Pavlova, "came to Russia and brought freedom to us all."

Pavlova was not the only member of Russia's ballet world to be affected by Duncan's unique concept of the dance. Both Michel Fokine, the brilliant, 29-year-old choreographer of the

Anna Pavlova performs The Dying Swan, *choreographer Michel Fokine's celebrated 1905 ballet. The ballerina's undulating arm movements were strongly influenced by Isadora Duncan's dancing.*

Imperial Ballet, and impresario Sergey Diaghilev were bowled over by Duncan. "Isadora," wrote Diaghilev many years later, "gave an irreparable jolt to the classic ballet of imperial Russia."

Michel Fokine agreed. "Duncan was the greatest American gift to the art of the dance," he said many years later. "She proved that all the primitive, plain, natural movements—a simple step, run, turn on both feet, small jump on one foot—are far better than

Their Grecian-style costumes reminiscent of Duncan's garb, Michel Fokine and his wife, Vera Fokina, dance the title roles in Fokine's 1912 ballet, Daphnis and Chloe.

all the richness of the ballet technique, if to this technique must be sacrificed grace, expressiveness, beauty."

Fokine, wrote Diaghilev, was "mad about" Duncan, whose influence "was the foundation of all [Fokine's] creation." Fokine began to introduce natural movement into ballet after he saw Duncan dance in St. Petersburg. Following her lead, he dispensed with the use of toe shoes and instructed his dancers to use their entire bodies when they moved. His artistically daring work had a powerful effect on modern ballet; his *Les Sylphides* would become the most frequently performed ballet of the 20th century.

Duncan followed her St. Petersburg triumph with brief appearances in the Russian cities of Kiev and Moscow, where riots were barely avoided as mobs of students struggled to see her. Then she returned to Berlin—to her new school, to her mother and sister, and to Gordon Craig.

The original plans for Duncan's school, which she envisioned as "a real children's paradise," had called for the enrollment of 40 girls, none of whom would pay tuition. She was making a very good income from her frequent stage appearances, but she soon realized that even that was not enough to feed, clothe, and educate so many children. Reducing the number of places to 20, she announced the school's opening. The school's "serious purpose," she said, was "to rediscover in its ideal form the beautiful rhythmic movements of the human body, in harmony with the highest beauty of physical form."

The reaction was overwhelming. Delighted by the prospect of a free education, hundreds of parents brought their little girls to Duncan's yellow house; a few children were even left on her doorstep. She finally selected 20 girls between the ages of 4 and 8 and, with the assistance of her sister, Elizabeth, began to teach them to dance. All pupils at the Isadora Duncan School wore the same "uniform": tunic and sandals.

The Duncans and the group of talented friends who volunteered to help them taught music, art, and standard school subjects, but the school's main emphasis was on gymnastics. Classes included acrobatics and practice in such natural movements as walking, marching, running, skipping, and jumping—all performed to rhythms that became gradually more complex. Duncan's goal was to train the children to move instinctively, so that they could ultimately "forget" their bodies and through them, "express the thoughts of the soul."

In July 1905, after her school had been in operation for several months, Duncan decided to introduce a group of her pupils at a recital in Berlin's Royal Opera House. Dressed in their short white tunics, their legs and feet bare, the girls performed a simple waltz. Gordon Craig later wrote that the performance of Duncan's "little flock" was "irresistibly lovely," but not everyone in Berlin agreed. Several prominent women, shocked by the exposure of "children's bare limbs," denounced Duncan as "immoral."

Britain's prim Queen Victoria had been dead for four years, but in 1905, the repressive atmosphere of the Victorian era still prevailed in much of the world. Disapproval of Duncan, increased by her unconcealed love affair with Gordon Craig, began to spread among the more straitlaced members of Berlin society. Finally, a group of women who had agreed to help support Duncan's school resigned. They could, they said, "no longer be patronesses of a school where the leader had such loose ideas of morals."

Furious, Duncan responded by hiring the Berlin Philharmonic Hall and giving a speech. She began lecturing about "the dance as an art of liberation," but ended up, she recalled in her autobiography, "with a talk on the right of woman to love and bear children as she pleased." As her audience sat in astonished silence, Duncan made clear exactly what she thought about marriage and women's rights.

"Truth and mutual faith," she said, were "the first principles of love," but most women married only to guarantee support for themselves and their children. Why, she asked, should a woman marry "a man who she thinks is so mean that, in case of a quarrel, he wouldn't even support his own children?"

Duncan said that "as a wage-earning woman," she would never "make the great sacrifice of strength and health and even risk my life to have a child" if "on some future occasion, the man can say that the child belongs to him by law." Concluding her fiery speech, she said, "Any intelligent woman who reads the marriage contract, and then goes into it, deserves the consequences."

Duncan's words caused an uproar.

Duncan was drawn, sculpted, painted, and photographed by dozens of artists. This drawing of the dancer, viewed from the wing of the stage, was made by Gordon Craig in 1905.

"Half of the audience sympathized with me," she recalled, "and the other half hissed and threw anything that came to their hands onto the stage." Although many people stormed out, a few remained to argue with Duncan. "We had," she noted, "an interesting debate on the rights and wrongs of women, which was considerably in advance of the Women's Movement of the present day." (By "present day," Duncan meant 1927, the year she wrote her autobiography. Radical even then, her views had been truly revolutionary in 1905.)

Duncan would soon have the chance to prove she meant what she said about having children: Less than a year after her impassioned speech at Philharmonic Hall, she discovered she was pregnant. She was delighted. Deeply in love with Gordon Craig, she had been hoping for a child since the early days of her relationship with him. Neither had the slightest interest in marrying.

She kept up her routine of European tours until she felt too awkward to dance. Then she settled down to wait for the baby in a small rented house in Holland. Her mother had returned to the United States, and Duncan had no desire to stay in Berlin as an object of public scorn. The months in her seaside cottage, however, were not happy ones for her.

Craig, who was deeply immersed in

Duncan, who had written, "I hope we'll have a dear sweet lovely baby and I'm happy forever," in an early letter to Craig, awaits the birth of their child in 1906.

A beaming Duncan cradles her daughter Deirdre, born in September 1906. Duncan compared childbirth with "the Spanish Inquisition," but she said motherhood made her feel like "a god."

his theatrical productions, visited her only occasionally. Lonely and worried that she might permanently lose the strength she needed for her career, Duncan went through a period of deep depression, even telling friends she was considering suicide. But on September 24, 1906, her gloom changed to joy when she gave birth to a daughter. As soon as he heard the news, Craig rushed to her side. He found her glowing with happiness.

"Oh, women, what is the good of us learning to become lawyers, painters, or sculptors, when this miracle exists? Now I know this tremendous love, surpassing the love of man," wrote the ecstatic new mother. "Oh, where was my art? My art or any art? I felt I was a god, superior to any artist."

A "god" she might be, but Isadora Duncan would dance for the rest of her life. Two months after the birth of her baby, named Deirdre, she was back at work. "I slipped into my old dresses and my old dances like a charm," she wrote later. "I suddenly felt myself dancing like a miracle."

Deirdre Duncan (left), the six-year-old daughter of Isadora Duncan and Gordon Craig, shares her mother's embrace with two-year-old Patrick, Duncan's son by millionaire Paris Singer, in 1912.

FIVE

Joy and Sorrow

Gordon Craig was the great love of Isadora Duncan's life, but her relationship with him was always stormy. In the months following the birth of their daughter, Deirdre, it got worse. Passionately dedicated to each other, both lovers were also demanding, stubborn, and intensely committed to their arts. By 1907, it was clear that they were headed for a final break.

"I had arrived at that frenzied state," wrote Duncan in her autobiography, "when I could no longer live with [Craig] or without him. To live with him was to renounce my art, my personality, nay, perhaps, my life, my reason itself. To live without him was to be in a continual state of depression, and tortured by jealousy." Many years later, Craig wrote, "I loved her—I do still—but she, the complex she, might have wrecked me."

Duncan not only had problems with Craig but financial worries as well. Her performances were her only source of income, but her pregnancy had kept her inactive for months. Still, she had to support herself and Deirdre, her school and all its pupils, and, frequently, Craig, whose expenses far surpassed his earnings.

The school, her most cherished project, was also her most expensive. In Russia, the government supported the Imperial Ballet School; why, she asked herself, should the Duncan School not also qualify for a government subsidy? The children, whose public appearances had been enthusiastically greeted by the public, could help. "I conceived the idea," she wrote later, "of taking them with me to different countries, in order to see if there were a single government which

61

Kaiserin Augusta Victoria, the wife of German ruler William II, was a strict defender of old-fashioned values. Duncan knew better than to seek her aid in obtaining government support.

would . . . give me the chance I needed to experiment with my project on a larger scale."

The German government, she decided, was hopeless. Her feminist views, her attire, and her liaison with Craig had already tarnished her reputation among many upper-class Germans, and the birth of her "love child" had dimmed it even more. Furthermore, the wife of the German kaiser (ruler) was well known for her prudish

attitudes, and extremely unlikely to favor government support for a school such as Duncan's. The *kaiserin*'s views, noted Duncan, "were so puritanical that when she visited a sculptor's studio, she sent her [servants] ahead to cover all the nude statues with sheets."

It was not surprising, then, that when Duncan was offered a contract for a Russian tour in 1908, she signed it quickly. Dora Duncan had come back to Europe; leaving the baby in her mother's care, Isadora Duncan once again set out for St. Petersburg. Accompanying her were 12 girls from her school, her sister, Elizabeth, and a governess. Her departure marked the end of her love affair with Craig, but she continued to care about him deeply, and she would make continual efforts to advance his career.

The Grand Duchess Olga, sister of the czar, sponsored the St. Petersburg recital of Duncan and her young dancers. The glittering audience at the Maryinsky Theater applauded and cheered the troupe, but the performance did not bring an offer of assistance from the czar. Russians saw Duncan's work as original, interesting, even beautiful—but not as part of the ballet tradition. Duncan went on to Moscow, where she met Konstantin Stanislavsky, founder of the famed Moscow Art Theater.

Stanislavsky, one of the giants of 20th-century theater history, was an actor, producer, and director. Among his contributions to the theater was the development of "method acting," now studied in drama schools all over the world. Before he introduced his revolutionary approach, actors played their roles in a stilted, artificial manner. Stanislavsky taught them to identify with the characters they were playing, to act with natural, human emotion.

The Russian theatrical pioneer and the innovative American dancer found they had much in common. "We understood each other almost before we had said a word to each other," recalled Stanislavsky in his 1924 autobiography, *My Life in Art*. In her own way, Duncan had long practiced "the method," emotionally identifying with the roles she was dancing. Stanislavsky, she said, helped her refine her technique. "Today, I worked all morning and put many new ideas into my work. Rhythms again," she wrote in a letter to him. "It is you who have given me these ideas. I am so glad I feel like flying to the stars and dancing round the moon."

In turn, Stanislavsky learned from Duncan. "Before I go out on the stage," he remembered her saying, "I must place a motor in my soul. When that begins to work, my legs and arms and my whole body will move independently of my will." Stanislavsky said that "at that time I was in search of that very creative motor, which the

Konstantin Stanislavsky (center) performs in Maksim Gorky's The Lower Depths *at the Moscow Art Theater in 1902. A pioneer of modern theater, Stanislavsky was one of Duncan's strongest Russian supporters.*

actor must learn to put in his soul before he comes out on the stage.... Comparing what she did to what I was doing, it became clear to me that we were looking for one and the same thing in different branches of art."

Stanislavsky did his best to help Duncan obtain government backing for

63

Sternly denouncing Duncan for dancing to classical music, Russian composer Nikolay Rimsky-Korsakov helped block government aid for her school.

her school, but it never materialized. If she had been supported by Russia's composers and musicians, she might have succeeded, but most of them were suspicious of her work. The Russian ballet had always been performed to specially composed—although often undistinguished—music, but Duncan danced to classical masterpieces.

Nikolay Rimsky-Korsakov, whose works include "The Flight of the Bumble Bee," was among the composers who felt that Duncan diverted attention from their music. "What repels me in her," he said, "is that she foists her art upon and tacks it onto musical compositions. . .whose authors do not at all need her company." Because of Duncan's influence, the Russian ballet eventually adopted the use of classical music—including some by Rimsky-Korsakov—but in 1908, the concept was too radical for the Russian people.

Undiscouraged, Duncan took her troupe to London. Once again she and her pupils received popular acclaim ("We have never seen such joy of life as we have seen in these children," commented one critic), but no offers of financial aid. And once again, Duncan was almost penniless. When her new manager, American Charles Frohman, offered her a contract for a tour of the United States, she gladly accepted.

Duncan wrote that it cost her "many pangs" to part with her daughter—now "a blond, rosy-cheeked child with blue eyes"—and her pupils, but she decided the children had traveled enough for the moment. Under the care of her sister, Elizabeth, she sent them to stay at the home of a friend near Paris.

"And so it happened that one day in July [1908], I found myself all alone on a big ship bound for New York—just eight years since I had left there on a cattle boat," wrote Duncan later. "I was already famous in Europe. I had created an Art, a School, a Baby. Not so bad. But, as far as finances went, I was not much richer than before."

At first, Duncan's reappearance in her native land was, as she put it herself, "a flat failure." Although some reports about her successes in Europe had reached the United States, most theatergoers knew little or nothing about her work. Charles Frohman booked her into a Broadway theater, backed her with a small, second-rate orchestra, and then failed to publicize her.

Opening during a record August heat wave, Duncan faced a near-empty theater. Reviewers either ignored her or patronized her with faint praise. The daily show-business newspaper, *Variety*, for example, called her movements "exquisitely graceful" but said "one could no more call [her performance] an entertainment than a public-school lecture on Egyptology."

Although the general public showed not the slightest interest in Duncan's work, she did attract the attention of New York's artistic community. An ardent following among a handful of sculptors, painters, and poets, however, was not enough to support a theatrical presentation, and at last, Frohman gave up. "Your art," he told Duncan, "is considerably over the heads of Americans, and they will never understand it. It would be better for you to return to Europe."

Duncan had a six-month contract with Frohman that guaranteed her a minimum payment, but she tore it up, freed him from his responsibility to her, and prepared to leave the country. She was persuaded to postpone her departure by her new artistic friends. They insisted, she recalled later, that it would be "a great sorrow" if she did not give her native land another chance to "appreciate her art."

She rented a New York studio and began to offer the same kind of private performances she had often given in Europe. She acquired, as she always did, a circle of enthusiastic admirers, but she still felt no closer to her goal. She had failed to acquire financial backing in Germany, in Russia, and in England. Now, in the United States, all she had to show for her efforts was a small clique of friends.

Then a new visitor began to appear at her "evenings." He was Walter Damrosch, conductor of one of the world's most important orchestras, the New York Symphony. Damrosch, who was probably the best-known and most popular classical musician in the United States, was deeply impressed by Duncan's art. He told her he would like to collaborate with her on a series of concerts at the Metropolitan Opera

Duncan's students, identically dressed in "pillbox" hats and braid-trimmed coats, gather for a group portrait in 1908. Standing at center is Duncan's favorite student, Irma.

House. He would lead the great, 80-piece orchestra; she would dance to the music of Beethoven and Richard Wagner. Duncan, as she said later, "joyfully assented."

The Damrosch-Duncan performances premiered at the Metropolitan Opera House in November 1908. This time the house was sold out. Duncan gleefully noted that even Charles Frohman, "who had sent for a box, was astonished to learn that not a seat remained in the theater." And this time, audiences and critics sang Dun-can's praises. Following their hugely successful debut, the orchestra and dancer toured several American cities, including Washington, D.C.

There Duncan was met, she said later, "by a perfect storm." Told that her unconventional behavior and scanty attire had created a "scandal" in Europe, a group of important government officials tried to prevent her appearance in the nation's capital. They failed, and the performance went on as scheduled, earning waves of applause from an audience that included the president of the United States, Theodore Roosevelt.

"He seemed to enjoy the performance and led the applause after every item of the program," observed Duncan with pleasure. In a letter to a friend, Roosevelt later commented: "What harm can these ministers find in Isadora's dances? She seems to me as innocent as a child dancing through the garden in the morning sunshine and picking the beautiful flowers of her fantasy."

Duncan, of course, was delighted to have at last gained recognition in her native land. She was also pleased with the "goodly deposits" that had begun to swell her bank account. In fact, she said later, "If it had not been for the pulling at my heartstrings to see my baby and my school, I would never have left America." But she had not seen Deirdre for six months; early in January 1909, she sailed for France.

Walter Damrosch conducts a military orchestra in New York City. Duncan's 1908 American tour, a failure until she met Damrosch, ended in triumph when she collaborated with the great conductor in a series of concerts.

Duncan arrived in Paris full of energy and optimism. After a "splendid reunion" with her daughter, she rented two huge apartments—one for herself and Deirdre, one for her pupils—and prepared to give a series of concerts at the Gaiété Lyrique, one of finest theaters in Paris. Parisians flocked to her performances, convincing her, she wrote later, that her dream of opening a new school was "within easy reach."

The toast of Paris in the spring of 1909, Duncan was earning an impressive income, but even this was not enough to finance a school on the scale she envisioned. She often talked to her sister, Elizabeth, about her need for a new source of income. "This can't go on!" she recalled joking. "My banking account is overdrawn. We must find a millionaire!"

And one day he materialized: a tall, blond, bearded man who introduced himself as Paris Eugene Singer. In her autobiography, Duncan recalled that Singer appeared in her dressing room

Isadora Duncan and Paris Singer share an affectionate moment in 1916. Singer, who was rich, generous, and utterly captivated by Duncan, had begun to support her and her students in 1909.

after a performance and said, "You do not know me, but I have often applauded your wonderful art." His words were to signal a new chapter in the life of 31-year-old Isadora Duncan.

Singer, 42 years old, was indeed a millionaire; he was the son of Isaac Merrit Singer, the fabulously wealthy inventor of the Singer sewing machine.

Named for the city in which he was born, Paris Singer was an American citizen who had been educated in England. He was handsome, charming, generous—and head over heels in love with Isadora Duncan. Events moved swiftly after their first meeting.

Singer was not particularly interested in dance or other arts, but he was eager to please this beautiful woman. When he learned that what she wanted most was to establish a school in which girls would be taught to "worship beauty," he offered to begin by sending her and "all these dancing children to a little villa on the Riviera [on the southern coast of France]," where they could "compose new dances." Duncan quoted him as saying, "The expense you don't need to worry about. I will bear it all. You have done a great work; you must be tired. Now let it rest on my shoulders."

It was a difficult offer to resist. Duncan and her pupils were soon established in a large house in the south of France, where Singer continued to shower them with kindness. "His devotion to [the children]," Duncan later recalled, "added a new element of trust to the feeling of gratitude with which I already regarded him, and which... was soon to deepen into something much stronger."

Singer next invited Duncan and her daughter on a cruise of the Mediterranean on his huge yacht. Leaving her

Back in Paris in the spring of 1909, Duncan lectures a group of her students on the dance. "My children!" she once wrote, "How could I hope to revive the lost art of dancing without their help?"

pupils in the care of governesses, she "sailed away toward Italy." Aboard the boat, the conservative millionaire and the radical dancer became aware of the many differences in their philosophies of life. "This man, who had declared that he loved me for my courage and generosity," wrote Duncan later, "became more and more alarmed when he found what sort of a red-hot revolutionary he had taken aboard his yacht."

At first Duncan was distressed by what she saw as Singer's typically "rich man's" attitudes. Aboard his boat, she recalled later, "I was unpleasantly aware of the stokers, stoking in the engine room, and 50 sailors on the

yacht; the captain and the mate—all this expenditure for the pleasure of two people."

Duncan "prattled on," she wrote in her autobiography, "explaining to [Singer] my ideas about life, Plato's *Republic*, Karl Marx [author of *The Communist Manifesto*], and a general reform of the world." But by now she, too, was in love. "I consoled myself with the idea that soon he would open his eyes and see, and that then he would help me to make that great school for the children of the people," she wrote.

With Singer, who continued to be generous and receptive to her ideas, Duncan and Deirdre settled down in a

Barefoot and wearing a Grecian-style toga and headband like her mother's, four-year-old Deirdre Duncan stands at the rail of Paris Singer's yacht during a 1910 trip to Egypt.

them," she would confess in her autobiography.

Duncan made a brief tour of Russia in the fall of 1909, and she continued to give occasional performances in Paris. But she also continued to brood about her luxurious new life-style. One day, as she watched Deirdre play on the beach outside an elegant hotel in Venice, Italy, where they were vacationing, she confronted her doubts. "Suddenly I began to suffer an intense nostalgia for my art—my work—my school," she recalled in her autobiography. "This human life seemed so heavy beside my dreams of art."

Duncan had a special reason for such thoughts: She had just discovered that she was pregnant with Singer's child. Having a baby would mean a painfully long absence from the stage, but she had strong maternal feelings. "Taking Deirdre in my arms," she wrote, "I whispered to her: 'You will have a little brother.'" When she told Singer about the news, he was, reported Duncan, "delighted—full of joy, love, tenderness."

A few weeks later Duncan and Singer sailed for the United States, where she had committed herself to a series of concerts with Walter Damrosch and the New York Symphony. The performances were sold out, but halfway through the tour, Duncan realized her pregnancy was becoming highly visible. In her autobiography, she wrote of a woman who came up to her after

large house in Paris. The dancer was soon at home in the world of the wealthy and privileged; at Singer's insistence, she even agreed to change her trademark style of dressing. "I, who had always worn a little white tunic, woollen in winter, linen in summer, succumbed to the enticement of ordering beautiful gowns, and wearing a performance and told her she should not dance in her "delicate" condition. "But that's just what I mean my dancing to express—Love—Woman—Formation—Springtime," she replied. "Botticelli's picture, you know.... Everything rustling, promising new life."

Nevertheless, Duncan knew it was time to stop. She canceled the rest of the tour and returned to France with Singer. After a midwinter cruise on the Nile River in Egypt, the couple took a huge house on the French Riviera. There, reported Duncan, "on the first day of May [1910], a morning when the sea was blue, and the sun was burning, and all Nature bursting into blossom and joy, my son was born."

With Patrick, a blond, blue-eyed, healthy baby, Duncan, Singer, and Deirdre returned to Paris. That summer, recalled Duncan, Singer "took it into his head that we should be married." Once again, she explained her views. "As I must spend my life making tours round the world, how could you spend your life in the stage-box admiring me?" she asked.

Singer replied that if Duncan were married she would not have to tour; she could live with him in England. He suggested that they try English country life for three months. Duncan was skeptical, but she agreed to spend the summer at Singer's vast estate in Devonshire. The experiment was not a success. It seemed to Duncan that the British gentry did nothing but eat,

Duncan, now wearing fashionable, contemporary clothing—and pregnant with Singer's child—rides an Egyptian donkey in the winter of 1910. Patrick Duncan was born a few months later.

write letters, take naps, and play bridge. "In the course of a couple of weeks," she recalled later, "I was positively desperate."

The summer in England, she wrote, "proved to me that I certainly was not suited to domestic life.... For the hundredth time, I made a firm decision that hereafter I would give my entire life to art." In the fall, "somewhat wiser

Upper-class Britons enjoy a day at the races. Hoping Duncan would learn to like English country life, Singer persuaded her to spend a summer engaged in such pastimes. She hated every minute of it.

found in children [whose movements are] more beautiful than any string of pearls belonging to any of the women who generally sit in the boxes here."

Admiring Americans packed the theaters where she danced, but they were unresponsive to her pleas for financial support. They had, after all, never seen any of her young pupils perform, and her fund-raising style was hardly a masterpiece of tact. One New York City newspaper summed it up with the headline, "Isadora Insults the Rich."

Completing her American tour, Duncan returned to her children, who had been staying with their governess at Singer's apartment. She resumed her relationship with Singer, but they began to have frequent disagreements. She said he was insensitive to art; he accused her of deliberately provoking him and flirting with other men. More and more often, he packed his bags and left for prolonged trips abroad.

Duncan cared deeply for Singer, but his frequent absences were more than compensated for by the presence of the two people she loved most in the world: Deirdre and Patrick. Duncan adored observing her little girl as she danced alone, unaware that anyone could see her. "Watching her exquisite grace and beauty," wrote her mother, "I dreamed that she, perhaps, would carry on my school as I imagined it. She was my best pupil." And Patrick, she observed, was also beginning to

and sadder," she sailed for America alone.

Singer had been generous, but he had not provided funds for the Paris school Duncan yearned to open. On her 1910 U.S. tour, therefore, she began to appeal to her audiences for funds. She addressed these wealthy, bejeweled theatergoers in typically frank, Duncanesque language. "No need for all those ornaments and fal-lals," she would say. "Fine art comes from the human spirit and needs no externals. . . . If my art has taught you anything here, I hope it has taught you that. Beauty is to be looked for and dance, "to a weird music of his own." Refusing to let his mother instruct him, he would say, "Patrick will dance Patrick's own dance alone."

Hating to be separated from her children, Duncan kept her travels to a minimum, but she wanted and needed to continue dancing. After making a brief tour of Russia early in 1913, she returned to Paris at the same time as Singer, who had spent the previous four months in Egypt. Duncan was pleased when Singer asked to see her and the children. "I loved him always," she wrote, "and longed to show him his own son, who had grown strong and beautiful in his father's absence." (Patrick was now almost three years old.) Singer, she knew, also "tenderly loved" Deirdre, who would be seven years old the following September.

After the four had a happy reunion lunch, Singer suggested that they all go for a ride in his car. The children, however, were scheduled for a music lesson, and Duncan was due at a rehearsal, so they made plans to meet later in the day. Deirdre, Patrick, and their governess climbed into the car to return home.

Duncan went back to her studio to rest before her rehearsal. In her autobiography, she described what happened next: "I was thus lazily eating sweets and smiling to myself, thinking '[Singer] has returned, all will be well,' when there came to my ears a strange, unearthly cry. I turned my head. [Singer] was there staggering like a drunken man. His knees gave way—he fell before me—and from his lips came these words: 'The children—the children—are dead!' "

The car had stalled on the way home, and the driver had gotten out to crank it up. Suddenly, the vehicle had jumped to life and begun to roll toward the Seine River. Unable to catch up with it, the driver had watched in horror as the car plunged into the deep, murky water. Passersby dove into the river, but no one could save the car's occupants. By the time the police arrived, the children and their governess had drowned.

Duncan later said that when she heard the agonizing news, she did nothing. "A strange stillness came upon me," she wrote, "only in my throat I felt a burning, as if I had swallowed some live coals." Her next reaction was to tell Singer calmly that the news could not possibly be true. Then, she said, she "felt an immense desire to comfort everyone." Was it, she wondered, "that I knew that death does not exist—that those two little cold images of wax were not my children, but merely their castoff garments? That the souls of my children lived on in radiance, but lived forever?"

All Paris—indeed, all the world— was racked with sympathy for Duncan. Thousands of letters and telegrams of

Mute testimony to tragedy, Paris Singer's car lies half submerged at the edge of the Seine. The vehicle's occupants—Duncan's children and their nurse—had drowned when it plunged into the river.

A flower-banked hearse carries Deirdre and Patrick Duncan's bodies through the somber streets of Paris. The children died in the spring of 1913.

condolence poured in, and crowds of silent, weeping Parisians stood watch over her house. Devastated, Singer collapsed and was taken to the hospital. Duncan, who could not bear the thought of putting her beloved children "in the earth to be devoured by worms," ordered that their bodies be cremated.

Duncan was grateful for the flood of sympathetic letters, but she could bring herself to read only a few of them. One, which she kept all her life, was from Gordon Craig, Deirdre's father. Enclosed with it was a tiny note that read, "Isadora, there is much to do. 1913." Craig knew that it would be very hard for Duncan to believe there was anything left to live for.

After the public mourning was over, Duncan's grief broke over her in a great wave, immobilizing her. Writing about this terrible time many years later, however, she said the outpouring of love from friends all over the world "helped me to realize what alone could comfort me—that all men are my brothers, all women my sisters, and all children on earth my children."

Inconsolable after her children's death, Duncan was nevertheless appalled to learn that Singer's chauffeur had been arrested. He was released after she appealed to the public prosecutor.

Raymond, the "most Greek" of the Duncan clan, plays a lyre shortly before going to Greece with his sister Isadora in 1913. Looking on are his wife, Penelope, and their son, Menalkas.

SIX

War and Work

After the tragic deaths of her children, Isadora Duncan, 36 years old, felt that her life was over. Hoping to distract her from her grief, her brother Raymond asked her to join him on an expedition to Greece, where he had volunteered to aid the victims of a recent war.

She agreed, but neither the work nor the change of scene helped her. In Greece, she wrote later, "All nature was glad and smiling, but I could find no comfort in it." She spent several weeks sitting on the shore, staring out to sea in silence. "I had entered a dreary land of grayness where no will to live or move existed," she wrote. "I sat and longed for annihilation and death."

When Singer learned that Duncan was in Greece, he joined her, but the intensity of her sorrow was too much for him. "One morning," she recalled

later, "he left abruptly, without warning. I saw the steamer receding over the blue waters and I was left once more alone." Realizing that she was of little use to her brother in his war-relief efforts, she soon left Greece herself, driving restlessly from Switzerland to France, then to Italy.

"I spent one night in Florence, where I knew Craig was living," she wrote later, "and I felt a great desire to send for him, but knowing he was now married and settled down to a domestic life. . . . I refrained." Duncan next went to visit an old friend in the small Italian town of Viareggio. There she met a sympathetic young sculptor. "Why are you always weeping?" she recalled his asking her. "Is there nothing I can do to help you?"

Duncan, who had been imagining that she saw Deirdre and Patrick, was

Actress Eleonora Duse, an old friend of Duncan, invited the bereaved dancer to visit her in Viareggio, Italy, in 1913. It was here that Duncan met the young sculptor who fathered her third child.

starting to feel that she had "one foot over the line which divides madness from sanity." In the company of the young sculptor, she slowly began to recover her self-confidence. "I felt I was rescued from grief and death, brought back to light—to love again," she later wrote of her brief affair with him. Not long afterward, she discovered that she would no longer be alone: She was pregnant. "From this moment," she wrote, "I entered into a phase of intense mysticism. I felt that my children's spirits hovered near me—that they would return to console me on earth."

She returned to Paris, where Singer was waiting for her with a gift. He had bought a large, elegant building, formerly a hotel, at Bellevue on the outskirts of Paris. He gave it to Duncan to use as a school and theater; with its 200 rooms, it could house many pupils and a large staff. She immediately began to transform the former hotel into what she called "a Temple of the Dance of the Future."

She conferred with architects, carpenters, painters. She hung her blue curtains in the old dining rooms, and selected 50 French children as her first students. Six teenage girls, who had been living with her when her children died, returned from Germany, where they had been staying with her sister, Elizabeth. Taking up residence at the new school, they became Duncan's teaching assistants. In January 1914, lessons at the school began.

Duncan's spirits revived rapidly in the next few months. "In the midst of this moving, bubbling life," she wrote, "I once more found the courage to teach, and the pupils learned with the most extraordinary rapidity." The future looked bright—but storm clouds were looming on the horizon.

By the summer of 1914, the political situation in Europe had become increasingly unstable. The continent was divided into rival groups of nations, each suspicious of the other, each poised to defend itself against any hostile move. Then, on June 28, Archduke Franz Ferdinand of Austria was assassinated by a Serbian terrorist. Austria-Hungary declared war on Serbia the next day, and within weeks, all the major powers of Europe were lined up on opposite sides. World War I had begun.

Because tension was increasing in Paris and her baby was soon due, Duncan sent her students to Singer's estate in England. On August 1, as the sound of guns and drums boomed through the open windows of the school, she gave birth to her third child, a boy. When she heard his first cries, she felt, she wrote later, "one great shock of joy." As for the approaching war, she thought, "My baby is here, safe in my arms. Now let them make war—what do I care?" Duncan's happiness, however, was short-lived. The baby died a few hours after birth.

Two days later, Germany declared war on France, which would soon become a great battlefield. Duncan was still recovering from the birth of her child when the French government asked for the use of her school as an emergency hospital. She quickly agreed. "Shortly after this," she recalled later, "I heard the first heavy steps of the stretcher-bearers, bringing in the wounded."

All over Europe, young men were

French soldiers await a German assault during World War I. Paris was filled with the sounds of battle when, on August 1, 1914, Duncan gave birth to her third child. He died soon after birth.

putting their peacetime lives aside and marching off to fight. Many would never return. To Duncan, her own pain seemed suddenly less significant. "What is one's personal sorrow when war—the disaster of either killing or maiming thousands—is mentioned?" she wrote.

When England entered the war, Singer decided his estate was no longer a safe place for Duncan's students. He sent them to the United States, where Duncan's sister and brothers took charge of them. The family urged Isadora Duncan to join them,

Duncan dances to "La Marseillaise," the French national anthem. Wildly applauded when it was introduced in New York City in 1914, "La Marseillaise" long remained one of Duncan's most popular works.

and in October 1914, she sailed for New York.

There she settled into a large studio, which quickly became a center for New York's artistic and literary society. The six older girls, who had now been with her for years, were so well trained in her method of dancing that they took almost complete charge of the younger pupils. They also began to make appearances with her. (Some years later, all six changed their last names to Duncan and became widely known by their nickname, "the Isadorables.")

Singer soon followed Duncan to New York; shortly after his arrival, he sponsored a concert for her at the Metropolitan Opera House. It would be Duncan's first public appearance since the death of Deirdre and Patrick, and she was struck with uncharacteristic stage fright beforehand. The performance was, however, a triumph. Opening with a dance performed to a requiem (funeral) march, she then danced to Schubert's "Ave Maria." Both men and women, aware of Duncan's recent tragedy, wept openly as she performed these two moving pieces.

At the end of the evening, she brought down the house when she wrapped herself in a bright red scarf and danced to the "Marseillaise," the national anthem of France. This dance, in fact, became one of the most celebrated selections in her repertoire. It

Attired in a Grecian-style gown and stylish straw hat, Duncan strolls through a Swiss garden with friends. She brought her students to neutral Switzerland in 1915.

was, she explained, "a call to the boys of America to rise and protect the highest civilization of our epoch—that culture which has come to the world through France."

Duncan's "Marseillaise" earned cheers from reviewers as well as from the audience. Critic Carl Van Vechten wrote, "Part of the effect is gained by gesture, part by massing of her body, but the greater part by facial expression, thereby arousing as vehement and excited an expression of enthusiasm as it would be possible for an artist to awaken in our theater today." Singer celebrated Duncan's Metropolitan appearance with a large dinner-dance at one of New York's most fashionable restaurants. Following the smashing success of the performance, the evening began in a festive mood, but it ended with one of the battles that had long been part of the Duncan-Singer relationship.

Singer had watched with mounting fury as Duncan danced ever more closely with an Argentinian partner. Finally, recalled a fellow guest, the angry millionaire "strode into the middle of the floor, took the Argentine by the scruff of the neck and slithered him out of the room." Equally furious, Duncan ripped off the diamond necklace Singer had given her, scattering the precious stones at his feet. Shouting, "I won't wear your diamonds!" she stormed out, starting another long period of estrangement from the devoted Singer.

Six months later, in May 1915, Duncan and her pupils returned to Europe. She borrowed money to support the girls, settled them in neutral Switzerland, then went back to live in Paris. As the war raged on, life in once sparkling Paris became increasingly dreary. The city was filled with refugees, lines of people waiting for scarce food supplies, and wounded soldiers. Every news report brought accounts of more battles, more men killed and wounded. Paris, said Duncan in a letter to a

Parisians inspect German bomb damage during World War I. As the conflict escalated, the mood of Paris became increasingly grim—an atmosphere, Duncan said, that matched her spirits.

friend, "is pretty sad but it suits my mood."

In this bleak world, Duncan's apartment was one small bright spot. As usual, her doors were always open to artists and intellectuals, and now to soldiers on home leave as well. When friends pointed out that she was spending more money on entertaining than she could afford, she shrugged and said "They were so hungry! It was the least I could do."

As well as helping to feed and amuse hordes of lonesome soldiers, Duncan volunteered her services to groups raising funds for war relief. She made her most spectacular contribution in the spring of 1916, when she performed at a charity event held at the huge Trocadero theater. This would be her first appearance in Paris since the death of her children; like their American counterparts, Parisians wept as they watched her dance to César

Wounded French soldiers arrive in Paris. Deeply moved by the pain and loneliness of the injured men who thronged the city, Duncan spent what little money she had to care for them.

Franck's "Redemption" and Pyotr Tchaikovsky's "Pathétique" (Sixth) Symphony.

As she had done in New York, she ended this performance with the "Marseillaise," receiving an even more tumultuous ovation. The song, after all, belonged to the French. As Duncan, dressed in a bright red tunic and accompanied by the distant sound of German artillery, danced out the anthem's lyrics, the entire audience rose to its feet and sang the stirring battle hymn.

The next day, a Paris newspaper critic described her performance. "In a robe the color of blood she stands enfolded," he wrote. "She sees the enemy advance; she feels the enemy as he grasps her by the throat; she kisses her flag; she tastes blood; she is all but crushed under the weight of the attack; and then she rises triumphant with the terrible cry, *Aux armes, citoyens!*

With the six students who had joined her in New York City, Duncan appears at Manhattan's Booth Theater in 1917. Known as the "Isadorables," the young women went on to successful dancing careers.

[Arm yourselves, citizens].... She does not make a sound.... but the hideous din of a hundred raucous voices seems to ring in our ears."

Duncan used no props, but spectators were so caught up in the dramatic performance that afterward, many of them thought she had been carrying a real flag. When she finished, the audience remained in place for more than an hour, applauding, cheering, and shouting for encores.

Meanwhile, the 23 Duncan students were still in Switzerland, where Dun-can had settled them to wait out the war—and Duncan was still responsible for their support. In May 1916 she decided to make a South American tour, hoping she could earn enough to pay the mounting bills in Switzerland. Her first stop was Buenos Aires, Argentina. There, things went wrong from the start.

Her baggage, which included her huge blue stage curtains and carpet, as well as the musical scores for the orchestra, was lost on the way. The local agent had failed to make any of the necessary arrangements for her scheduled performances. Most damaging, Duncan herself created a scene that outraged members of Buenos Aires society.

Soon after her arrival she visited a nightclub popular with the city's students. Here she danced the tango, which she described with characteristic verve: "I felt my pulses respond to the enticing, languorous rhythm of this voluptuous dance, sweet as a long caress, intoxicating as love under southern skies, cruel and dangerous as the allurement of a tropical forest."

Surrounded by wildly cheering students, Duncan next wrapped herself in Argentina's flag and danced to the music of its national anthem. The students loved it, but Argentinian society was shocked; after the next day's newspaper accounts of the gala evening, most of them boycotted Duncan's subsequent appearances. Duncan fared better with the public during the rest of the South American tour, but overall, the project was a financial failure.

With no funds to pay their bills, most of Duncan's students left Switzerland and returned to their homes. "This dispersing of the school to which I had sacrificed years of work," she wrote sadly, "cost me much pain, but I was somewhat comforted by the arrival [in New York] of the six elder children shortly afterwards."

Alone and almost penniless, Duncan went to New York in September 1916. When she landed, she telephoned her good friend Arnold Genthe, a prominent photographer. To her astonishment, the call was answered not by Genthe, but by someone even closer to her. It was Paris Singer, who by coincidence was visiting the photographer. "When he heard I was alone at the docks without funds," recalled Duncan, "he at once said he would come to my aid." The Singer-Duncan romance was on again.

For the next few months, Duncan stayed in New York, where she gave several concerts at the Metropolitan Opera House. Her most popular dance, especially after April 1917, when the United States entered the war on the side of England and France, was the "Marseillaise." When news of the Russian Revolution reached the United States in the spring of 1917, she fol-

By now acclimatized to the United States—and no longer limited to Grecian-style clothing—the Isadorables stroll confidently through Manhattan in 1917.

lowed the French anthem with a special dance dedicated to "all those who had suffered, been tortured, died in the cause of humanity."

Set to the music of Tchaikovsky's "Marche Slav," the dance celebrated the freeing of Russia's peasants from the tyranny of the czar. Describing her performance, one reviewer wrote, "Groping, stumbling, head bowed, knees bent, she struggles forward. . . . Finally comes the moment of release, and here Isadora brings [her hands] forward slowly and we observe with horror that. . . .after their long serfdom [slavery] they are not hands at all, but claws, broken, twisted. . . .The expression of frightened, almost uncompre-

The first Madison Square Garden (two other Manhattan sports arenas have since borne the name) was among the gifts Paris Singer offered Duncan. When she scornfully rejected it, he left her for good.

hending joy with which Isadora concludes the march is another stroke of her vivid imaginative genius."

Duncan, who had never forgotten the sight of the 1905 workers' funeral in St. Petersburg, was overjoyed by the success of the revolution. "In all my art career," she wrote later, "it has been these movements. . . .that have most attracted me. In my red tunic I have constantly danced the revolution and the call to arms of the oppressed."

Not all her wealthy admirers, however, shared her enthusiasm for the victory of communism in Russia; her

"revolutionary" dance, she noted, "raised some storm with the audience." Also well aware of Singer's disapproval of her politics, she wondered if, "watching me night after night from his box," he ever asked himself "whether this school of grace and beauty of which he was the patron might not become a dangerous thing that would lead him and his millions to annihilation."

Whatever he thought of her views on revolution, Singer was his usual freespending self; he established Duncan in a luxurious apartment, paid her bills in Switzerland, and, at her request, sponsored several free recitals in New York. When she complained of exhaustion, he sent her and his private secretary to Cuba for a vacation. Duncan had often been uneasy about accepting Singer's lavish gifts, but "for the time being," she wrote, "life became wonderful through the magic power of money."

Eager to "immortalize" her, Singer decided to endow a huge art center in New York City. The center, named for Duncan, would house a school and theater for her and provide facilities and performance space for artists, poets, and dancers. Excited by his plan, the millionaire made secret arrangements to buy Madison Square Garden, Manhattan's huge sports arena.

Singer decided to spring his surprise at a dinner party, to which he also invited Genthe, Augustin and Eliza-

The Isadorables perform in 1918 in Long Island, New York, without their teacher, who had returned to Paris. The open-air concert was staged to raise funds for war victims.

beth Duncan, and several other artists. Again, the occasion did not turn out as he expected. According to Duncan's memoirs, she "was enthusiastic about the plan as a whole," but "not in favor of starting so vast a project in the middle of the war." According to others present, however, she resented Singer's public announcement of his latest generosity and reacted to it with scornful anger.

Many years later, Victor Seroff, Duncan's close friend and author of a biography, *The Real Isadora*, talked to Genthe about what happened next. Duncan said, reported Genthe, "Do you mean to tell me that you expect me to direct a school in Madison Square Garden? I suppose you want me to advertise prize fights with my dancing."

"Singer turned absolutely livid," re-called Genthe. "His lips were quivering and his hands were shaking. He got up from the table without saying a word and left the room."

Genthe and the rest of the group were horrified. "Do you realize what you have done?" they asked. "You could have had the school that was your life's dream, and now you have ruined everything."

Duncan was unworried. "He'll come back," she said. "He always does." But, said Genthe, "He never did. She sent her brother, her sister-in-law, and finally the pupils to plead with him. He was adamant. Her letters to him went unanswered. All funds were stopped."

Duncan spent the rest of the summer in New York, entertaining and giving occasional recitals with her students. Although motion pictures had been popular in the United States for

Augustin Duncan, Isadora's older brother, was known to her students as "Uncle Gus." After she left the United States in 1918, he arranged a concert tour for the Isadorables.

A French officer thanks Duncan for permitting her school to be used as a wartime hospital and military base. She later sold the building, which was badly damaged, to the government.

more than a decade, Duncan had so far ignored the "vulgar" new medium. During the summer of 1917, she saw her first movie. To her surprise, she found it, as she told a friend, "more fun than I imagined." Nevertheless, she refused to sign any of the film contracts she was offered later, claiming that the flickering medium would make her art look like "a St. Vitus dance." She would, she said, "rather not be remembered like that for posterity."

In the fall, Duncan embarked on a tour of California. She had not visited her home state since leaving it 22 years earlier. She also visited her mother,

whom she had not seen for almost a decade. Dora Duncan had moved back to San Francisco soon after Deirdre's birth because, said her daughter, she was homesick. Other observers, however, believed it was Dora Duncan's disapproval of her daughter's highly unconventional life-style that led to the estrangement of the two women.

Duncan returned to Paris in March 1918, 10 months before the war finally ended. She had hoped to reopen her school there, but the building had been virtually destroyed by its wartime use. First serving as a French hospital, it had later been converted to an American army training base. Unable to use the dilapidated structure as it was and lacking the money to repair it, she sold it to the French government for a fraction of its original cost. Undaunted, she bought a small house near Paris and began to dance.

Now almost 40 years old, the formerly slim Duncan had grown rather heavy. As the result of her terrible sorrow, she had aged visibly. She had begun to dye her hair (which had turned white), but she looked older than she was. Still, however, she moved with astonishing lightness and grace; when she danced, her audiences forgot her age and weight.

Busy rebuilding the nation after four devastating years of war, the French government had no funds for dance schools. But still, Duncan refused to give up her dream. After a 1920 performance at the Champs Elysées Theater in Paris, she appealed to the audience once again. "Help me to get my school," she said. "If not, I will go to Russia with the bolsheviks. I know nothing of their politics. I am not a politician. But I will say to the leaders: 'Give me your children, and I will teach them to dance like gods.'"

A year later, she got the chance to make good on her threat. She was performing at the Prince of Wales Theater in London when she met a very important Russian official: Leonid Krasnin, head of the Soviet government's Trade Commission in London. When Krasnin came backstage to tell Duncan how much he had enjoyed her work, she told him about her desire to establish a school. Krasnin was interested.

The Soviet official discussed the idea with his colleagues in Moscow, who agreed that a school like the one Duncan proposed would be a great asset to their struggling new government. Soon after his first meeting with Duncan, Krasnin presented her with a contract. "A contract between comrades, what an utterly preposterous idea!" she replied. Instead, she wrote a letter containing her own framework for an agreement.

"I shall never hear of money in exchange for my work," it said. "I want a studio-workshop, a house for myself and my pupils, simple food, simple tunics, and the opportunity to give our best work.... I want to dance for the masses, for the working people who need my art and have never had the money to come to see me.... If you accept me on these terms, I will come and work for the future of the Russian Republic and its children."

When she returned to Paris, Duncan found a telegram from Anatoly Lunacharsky, the Soviet commissar of education. "Come to Moscow," it said. "We will give you school and thousand children. You may carry on your idea on a big scale." Duncan responded immediately. "Accept your invitation," she wired. "Will be ready to sail from London July first."

*Soviet education commissar Anatoly Lunacharsky welcomes Duncan to his country.
The commissar, who had been skeptical about Duncan's idealistic political statements,
was astonished when she showed up in Moscow.*

SEVEN

Russia

Duncan and her mother had planned a reunion in London, but the ship bringing Dora Duncan from America was delayed by a storm at sea, and the two missed each other. As it turned out, their 1918 meeting in San Francisco was their last. Bound for the Soviet Union, Duncan left England in July 1921. Sailing with her was Irma Duncan, one of the six young "Isadorables" who had adopted their teacher's name.

Duncan, who had always enjoyed having her fortune told, visited a gypsy crystal gazer before boarding her ship. "You are bound on a long journey," announced the fortune-teller. "You will have many strange experiences, you will have troubles, you will marry. . . ." Duncan, she later recalled, "cut her short with laughter. I, who was always against marriage? I would

never marry. The fortune-teller said, 'Wait and see.' "

In 1921, the Russian experiment with communism was in its early stages. The new form of government was violently opposed by many in the West, but Duncan, like many other optimists, thought it offered great hope for mankind. "I actually believed that the ideal state, such as Plato, Karl Marx, and Lenin had dreamed it, had now by some miracle been created on earth," she recalled later. "I was ready to enter the ideal domain of communism."

Her vision of utopia was modified soon after she arrived in the Soviet Union. The nation was still reeling from the effects of the 1917 revolution, which had overthrown a long-established way of life; with food, clothing, and housing in short supply, day-to-

This huge Moscow mansion was assigned to Duncan and her school by the Soviet government. She lost no time in furnishing the building with her familiar blue curtains and carpets.

day existence was chaotic. Education commissar Anatoly Lunacharsky had received Duncan's wire accepting his invitation, but, he said later, he had not really believed she would leave the comforts of life in western Europe for a spartan existence in postrevolutionary Russia. No one, therefore, met Duncan and Irma at the Moscow railroad station. No apartment and no school awaited them.

Finding suitable quarters in overcrowded Moscow was a major project, but Soviet authorities finally installed Duncan in an ornate mansion. The former residence of an aristocrat who had fled the country after the revolution, the house was now stripped of its elaborate furnishings; Duncan quickly installed simple, low couches and her

trademark blue curtains and carpets. Her needs, she said, were simple: "I want only black bread and *kasha* [cooked grain]," she told her hosts, "but I want 1,000 students."

In the end, she had to settle for 50 pupils, chosen from the hundreds who applied. Promised that more children would be enrolled later, she set to work. She taught by demonstration and by speaking in English, which was translated to her classes. On November 7, 1921, the fourth anniversary of the Russian Revolution, she and her school made their debut. It was an exciting event. Moscow's residents were eager to see this foreigner, whom local newspapers called the "world-famous artist who had courageously left a crumbling, capitalistic Western Europe" to throw in her lot with the "new world" of Soviet Russia.

On the night of the performance, the 3,000 seats of Moscow's Bolshoi Theater were filled, and the aisles were packed with people who could not find seats. In the audience was a very special viewer: Vladimir Ilich Lenin, father of the modern Soviet state. After dancing to Tchaikovsky's "Pathétique" Symphony, Duncan performed the "Marche Slav", her dramatic tribute to the revolution. Audiences in New York, Paris, and London had been excited by this work, but the people of Moscow were ecstatic. "It was not dancing in the ordinary technical sense," reported the official newspaper, *Izvestia*, the next day, "it was the most beautiful interpretation . . . of the revolution."

For her program's finale, Duncan danced to the *Internationale*, the Soviet national anthem. This time, said *Izvestia*, "the audience saw Irma Duncan come from a corner of the bare stage, leading a little child by the hand, who was followed in turn by another and another—a mass of children in red tunics moving against the blue curtains . . . surrounding with their youthful outstretched arms the noble, undaunted, and radiant figure of their teacher."

At this sight, continued the newspaper, "the audience sprang to its feet, and with one mighty voice sang fervently the words to their hymn." When the performance ended, the theater was rocked by applause and cheers; one of the loudest voices was that of Vladimir Lenin, shouting "Bravo, bravo, Miss Duncan!"

The evening at the Bolshoi was a triumph, but Duncan's satisfaction in it was short-lived. Soon afterward, Commissar Lunacharsky brought unwelcome news: The government had adopted a new economic policy that legalized the private buying and selling of goods and services. This meant, explained Lunacharsky, that Duncan would be permitted to sell tickets for her performances—and that the government would no longer provide financial support.

When Duncan came to the Soviet

Attended by Irma Duncan (left), Isadora Duncan marries Russian poet Sergey Yesenin on May 2, 1922. Duncan, almost 44, listed her age on the marriage certificate as 37; Yesenin was 27.

Union, she believed that here, in this new nation created for the common man, she would at last be able to concentrate on teaching her art to a whole generation of children. Now she was back where she had started. To operate the school of which she had dreamed for so long, she would have to devote her time to performing for money. Refusing to consider returning to the West, she arranged to give a series of concerts in Moscow; they proved to be sellouts, earning enough

ISADORA DUNCAN
IRMA DUNCAN AND CHILDREN OF HER SCHOOL IN MOSCOW.

Duncan lectures students at her Moscow school. She often took the youngsters to symphonic concerts and to the Moscow Art Theater, but she flatly refused to let them watch ballet.

money to buy food for the children and wood to heat the enormous house that sheltered them.

Duncan was disappointed by the loss of government sponsorship of her school, but she was cheered by the success of her concerts—and by the company of a new friend. At a Moscow party soon after Christmas, 1921, she met a Russian poet named Sergey Yesenin. Extremely popular in Moscow's artistic and intellectual circles, the handsome, blond Yesenin was a founder of the Imagists, a group of Russian poets whose work employed

striking, down-to-earth images. When he met the 43-year-old Duncan, Yesenin was 26. He spoke no English; she spoke only a few words of Russian. Nevertheless, the two were strongly attracted to each other; they soon began an intense relationship.

Yesenin enjoyed watching Duncan perform such pieces as the "Marche Slav," but he had no interest in classical music or theater. For her part, Duncan loved the "music" of Yesenin's poetry, but she did not understand its language, and she knew nothing about Russian literature. Writing about the couple years later, mutual friends recalled that Yesenin was drawn to Duncan by her vitality, her grace, and, undeniably, by her celebrity. She saw him both as a fiery genius and a good-looking, strong-willed young man who needed mothering. The life they began together—almost always with a translator in attendance—was predictably tumultuous.

Yesenin was charming, often expressing affection and admiration for Duncan. He was, however, jealous of her fame, which far outweighed his own. A heavy drinker, he sometimes said cruel and humiliating things to her in the presence of others. Lola Kinel, the young woman who served as the couple's translator, later recalled a painful conversation that was, perhaps, typical.

Yesenin, who had been drinking, smilingly told Duncan that "a dancer can never become very great because her fame doesn't last. People may come and admire you. . . . but after you are dead, no one will remember. But poets live. I, Yesenin, shall leave my poems behind me. . . . Poems like mine live forever."

At these words, said Kinel, "a shadow passed over Isadora's face." She said, "Tell him he is wrong, tell him he is wrong. I have given people beauty. I have given them my very soul when I danced. And this beauty did not die. It lives somewhere." Duncan, said Kinel, had "tears in her eyes" as she "added in her pitiful, childish Russian: 'Krasota nie umiray [beauty not die].' "

Duncan and Yesenin disagreed about many things, including fortune-telling and card reading. Duncan herself only half-believed in these superstitious practices, but she often experimented with them, particularly when she was tense or bored. In her autobiography, she reported that in April 1922, she and a friend were playing with a ouija board (a device that, some believe, can bring supernatural messages) when, suddenly, the letters D O R A appeared. Aware that her mother, who was staying with Raymond Duncan in Paris, had been ill, Duncan was alarmed by the "message." The next morning, her fears were confirmed by the arrival of a telegram from Paris; it announced that Dora Duncan had died on April 22.

Mother and daughter had been estranged for some time, but still, Duncan was devastated by the news. Wanting to leave for Paris at once, she asked government officials for her passport, which she had surrendered when she arrived in the Soviet Union. The document, however, had been misfiled, delaying her departure for weeks. By the time it was found, she had decided to go to the United States instead.

An American tour, she thought, would give her an opportunity to raise funds for her school. It would also give

Yesenin a chance to see some of the rest of the world. When she applied to Lunacharsky for a passport for Yesenin, however, she ran into a problem. The commissar told her that the Russian government placed "great value" on Yesenin. The poet would, he said, "be exposed to all sorts of dangers" if he traveled in a country where the Soviet Union had not yet been officially recognized.

Duncan, she recalled afterward, asked what she could do. "You are a world-famous artist," replied Lunacharsky. "Your name would be his protection—that is, if he were Isadora Duncan's husband." Duncan, who had called marriage "an impossible proposition for a free-spirited woman," had vowed she would never marry. Marriage however, seemed to offer fewer disadvantages in the Soviet Union than in the West. Here, it was a simple legal agreement, easily dissolved by either party on demand. On May 2, 1922, Isadora Duncan became the wife of Sergey Yesenin. The newlyweds arrived in New York City the following October.

Known as "the jazz age," the 1920s were years of sharply contradictory attitudes in the United States. Prohibition, which outlawed the sale or use of alcohol, was in effect; at the same time, Americans were consuming record amounts of liquor. Across the nation, "speakeasies" (illegal bars) flourished, and millions of people quietly made

Tennessee schoolteacher John Scopes (center) prepares for the 1925 event popularly known as the "Monkey trial." He stood accused of teaching his pupils that man's ancestors might have been apes.

their own gin and wine, or bought it from bootleggers.

America was a country where "flappers"—convention-defying, short-skirted, cigarette-smoking young women—and their nattily attired beaux danced the nights away to jazz bands. It was also the country where, in 1925, Tennessee schoolteacher John Scopes would be brought to trial and convicted of teaching evolution, a theory that outraged religious citizens who refused to believe that man developed from earlier, less complex forms of life.

Its victorious participation in World War I had made the United States a great international power, but by the

A curious crowd looks on as a U.S. government official destroys barrels of illegal beer during Prohibition. Alcoholic beverages were outlawed in the United States from 1920 to 1933.

Dancers demonstrate the Charleston, America's favorite step in the 1920s. The music of the decade was jazz, which Duncan detested. The idea that "jazz rhythm expresses America," she said, was "monstrous."

1920s, "isolationism"—a desire to withdraw from involvement with the rest of the world—was a strong force. Americans had become suspicious of all things foreign, particularly those that smacked of Russian "bolshevism."

When Duncan and Yesenin landed in New York, they were treated almost like spies by immigration officials. Suspecting that the couple carried material "pertaining to the overthrow of the American government," officials carefully examined every item in their baggage, even confiscating Duncan's musical scores and Yesenin's manuscripts. The artists were questioned about everything from their political opinions to their reasons for visiting the United States.

When they were finally released, Duncan and Yesenin were confronted by a crowd of eager reporters. Hurt and angry to be received this way in her own country, Duncan said, "I had absolutely no idea that the human mind could worry itself into figuring out all the questions that were rapidly fired at me today. I have never had anything to do with politics. . . . To say, or even hint, that I am a Bolshevik is rot. Rot! Rot!"

New Yorkers, many of whom were outraged by their country's treatment of Duncan, flocked to Carnegie Hall to see her first performance. Other successful New York appearances followed; after each, Duncan made a speech, appealing for support for her

Moscow school. The audiences here were friendly and responsive, but in Boston, where she next performed, it was another story.

Traditionally proper Bostonians were not enthusiastic about Duncan's costumes or about her praise for her husband's homeland. Incensed by their chilly reaction, Duncan addressed the crowd in what was later called an "inflammatory" manner. Under blazing headlines—"Red Dancer Shocks Boston; Duncan in Flaming Scarf Says She's Red"—the next day's newspapers carried the story. "She seized a red scarf attached to her costume," read one report, "incidentally and accidentally revealing more of her person than usual, and waved it over her head. 'This is red! So am I,' she cried. 'It is the color of life and vigor!' "

Boston's mayor reacted to Duncan's "disgraceful performance" by revoking her license to perform in the city. Many other communities followed suit by cancelling scheduled Duncan performances. She nevertheless toured the country, appearing in such cities as Chicago, Milwaukee, St. Louis, Memphis, Baltimore, and Philadelphia.

She created an uproar everywhere she went. Anticipating her arrival in his city, the mayor of Indianapolis issued a statement: "If she goes pulling off her clothes and throwing them in the air, as she is said to have done in Boston," he announced, "there's going to be somebody getting a ride in the [police] wagon." Billy Sunday, a well-known evangelist, made what was probably the most colorful denunciation of the unconventional dancer. "That bolshevik hussy," he shouted from his pulpit, "doesn't wear enough clothes to pad a crutch!"

Meanwhile, Yesenin was disgusted to find that no one in America had ever heard of him or his poetry. Galled by being identified only as "Isadora's husband," he tried to get attention by carrying a silver dagger and wearing flamboyant cloaks, boots, and huge fur hats. He began to drink heavily, often behaving abusively to his wife. Newspapers carried stories of drunken bouts in which he smashed hotel-room furniture and engaged in public brawls.

Duncan was exhausted by the barrage of sensational press reports, by the suspicious attitude of her fellow Americans, and by her husband's difficult behavior. Clearly, it was time to leave. After a final performance in New York's Carnegie Hall in January 1923, she and Yesenin sailed for France. Talking to reporters on shipboard, she said, "I am not an anarchist or a bolshevik. My husband and I are revolutionists. All geniuses worthy of the name are.... Goodbye, America. I shall never see you again."

In Paris, the couple checked into the luxurious Crillon Hotel, but the change of scene did not improve Yesenin's mood. Still drinking to excess, he en-

Evangelist Billy Sunday, who often emphasized his points by pounding on a Bible, warns his congregation about what he called the "sinful antics" of "that bolshevik hussy," Isadora Duncan.

gaged in more destructive acts, one of which virtually destroyed his elegant hotel room. Once again, splashy newspaper headlines told the story: "Isadora's Poet Stirs Riot in Paris Hotel," said one. Duncan, who later told a friend that she had "made a terrible mistake in taking [Yesenin] out of Russia," decided to take him home.

When Duncan and Yesenin got off the train in Moscow in August 1923, more than a year after their departure for the United States, Yesenin fell to his knees and kissed the ground. Nevertheless, he continued to stage stormy scenes with his wife. The couple was very low on funds, but at one point, Duncan realized that Yesenin had hidden thousands of dollars—of her money—in one of the many trunks he had brought back from the United

Eager to discredit press reports about Yesenin's drunken brawls and frequently abusive behavior, the poet and his wife strike an affectionate pose during a 1925 news conference.

States. The trunks, which Yesenin always kept locked, also proved to contain an enormous collection of expensive clothes and jewelry he had purchased secretly. Duncan's discovery triggered an especially ugly quarrel with Yesenin.

After this painful scene, Yesenin left home for several days. The couple reconciled, but Yesenin continued to drink heavily. His quarrels with his wife grew fiercer and his disappearances more frequent. At a boisterous party following a Bolshoi Theater performance in late 1923, Duncan touched her husband's arm, silently suggesting he had drunk enough. Furious, he slammed the glass on the table and walked out. Duncan never saw him again.

Her school continued to absorb all her thoughts. "They dance beautifully, but they are always hungry," Duncan said to a friend about her students. "However," she added, "they have great spirit. They live on *kasha* and black bread, but when they dance, you would swear they were fed on ambrosia." In order to keep them supplied even with black bread, Duncan spent the eight months after Yesenin's departure touring the Soviet Union. The school was left in Irma Duncan's care.

Duncan worked hard, traveling to such remote, uncomfortable cities as Tashkent and Samarkand, but the needed income was not to be found. In the provinces, she said later, "The working men, who had no money to buy tickets, insisted upon coming *free*, saying, as I was a communist, I should dance for all the comrades"—which, she said, she "would be very pleased to do" if she did not urgently need money for the school.

She finally returned to Moscow, where her school had been busy. Under Irma's tutelage but according to Duncan's plan, the 40 students had themselves been teachers, showing 500 workers' children how to dance as they had been taught.

When Duncan went out on the school's balcony, she saw hundreds of children below her, cheering. "Then the band struck up the *Internationale*," recalled Irma Duncan later, "and all the children danced past the balcony, each one holding high the hand of the comrade in front. Isadora wept to see them." She *was* bringing dance to a new world. The hardships had been worth it.

Once again, Duncan decided to go abroad, where her performances could help keep her school going. She left for Germany in the fall of 1924, but her bad luck dogged her there. In Berlin, the agent who had booked her appearances proved to be a swindler; he absconded with the proceeds from her well-attended concerts, leaving her with nothing to show for her work.

She tried to arrange for a series of performances in Czechoslovakia and Austria, but her well-known associa-

A trio of Duncan students—(left to right) Margot, Anna, and Irma Duncan—reflect their teacher's spirit as they join hands in an impromptu dance by the sea.

tion with the Soviet Union made her politically suspect, and she was unable to obtain entry visas for those countries. "I am living from hand to mouth," she said in a letter to Irma, "The joke of the whole thing is that it is current gossip that I receive vast sums from the Soviets. Isn't that beautiful?" Duncan, who kept writing to Irma, begging for news of her school and its pupils, was puzzled by Irma's failure to respond. (What she could not know was that Irma, her favorite student, had taken advantage of her teacher's absence to assume the directorship of the school herself.)

After several unhappy months in Berlin, Duncan managed to get to Paris, but at this point, her legendary energy and optimism were running low. Aging, growing heavy, sometimes drinking too much, she lacked both the spirit and the stamina to dance. Then, on New Year's Eve, 1925, she received tragic news: A telegram from the Soviet Union informed her that Sergey Yesenin had killed himself.

Soon afterward, in a letter to a friend, Duncan wrote, "Yesenin's death was a terrible blow to me, but I cried so much that I cannot suffer any more and I am so unhappy myself now that I often think of following his example, but in a different way. I would prefer the sea."

But Isadora Duncan was a fighter. Despite her occasional hints about suicide, she rarely indulged her depressions. She remained passionately committed to the school that she hoped to reestablish in Paris. She dreamed of bringing some of her Russian students to live with her there, to help her teach another generation of children to dance. She tried hard, but still she was unable to raise enough capital to realize her goal.

Duncan had often been approached by publishers who wanted to buy her memoirs, but she always insisted that she was a dancer, not a writer. In 1926, however, she decided that writing a book was the one way she could solve her financial problems. She signed a contract and began writing, usually delivering a few pages at a time to her agent. Her first few chapters were rejected as "too arty"; the public, she was told, wanted to hear less philoso-

phizing and more about her love life. Finally, she completed a satisfactory manuscript, which in 1927 was published under the title *My Life*.

In May that same year, Duncan turned 49. The following July, at an age when most dancers would have long since retired, she gave a major concert in Paris, dancing to the music of César Franck, Franz Schubert, and Richard Wagner. "Her interpretation of Franck's 'Redemption'," wrote one observer, "was monumental, and her 'Ave Maria,' with maternal arms lulling an imaginary babe, was so personal and so heartrending in its simplicity that it provoked unashamed sobs throughout the audience. At the end of the performance she was cheered and called back to the stage again and again."

Duncan was exhausted by the performance but elated by its success, and she immediately began to plan a series of new programs for the fall. Deciding to rest until then, she went to stay with friends in Nice, a French resort on the Mediterranean coast. There, on September 14, she spotted a bright red Italian sports car, a Bugatti, in a showroom window. Always fond of fast cars and fast driving, she told the automobile dealer she might be interested in buying the Bugatti. Could he, she asked, arrange for a demonstration? He could indeed; he would, in fact, send the car and a driver to pick her up that evening.

It was a cool night, and Duncan's

Wrapped in a long, red, fringed shawl, Duncan relaxes in her Paris apartment in 1920. It was this shawl, her favorite, that would prove to be the instrument of her death seven years later.

Raymond and Elizabeth Duncan attend the 1927 funeral of their sister Isadora in Paris. The dancer's body was cremated, its ashes interred with those of Deirdre and Patrick Duncan.

friends suggested that she wear a warm coat. Rejecting such an undramatic idea, she flung her red, fringed shawl around her neck, jumped into the low-slung vehicle, and struck a mock-heroic pose. "*Adieu, mes amis,*" she said theatrically, "*je vais à la gloire!*" (Farewell, my friends, I go to glory.)

The powerful little car sprang forward, then jerked to a halt. The driver was screaming.

Duncan's friends rushed to the car. There, to their horror, they saw that the fringe of her long red shawl was tightly entangled in the spokes of one of the wheels. Duncan's head was slumped on her chest; her neck was broken. She had died instantly.

Duncan's body was brought back to Paris, where it was to be cremated and interred with the ashes of her children. Soaked by steady rain, thousands of weeping mourners lined the route of the funeral procession as it wound its way toward the cemetery. During the final ceremony, a letter written by Duncan herself was read aloud.

"In a moment of clearsightedness and strength," it said, "we understand that even the worst afflictions, catastrophes, horrors, are but a veil of mystery hiding other truths. . . . I am going at once to start work, forward, always with the voices of the unseen angels, with beauty, the divine music, towards the joy and the light that are our final goal."

Duncan, who once said that the most "beautiful human being" was "a dancing child," welcomes visitors to the garden at her Paris school. Here, she said, she hoped "to awaken once more an art which has slept for 2,000 years."

EIGHT

Duncan's Legacy

It is hard to define, precisely, Isadora Duncan's artistic legacy. Certainly she gave the world a new vision of the dance, of the way that movement could convey human emotion. But as dance scholar Walter Sorell writes in his critical history, *Dance in Its Time*, Duncan contributed far more than the "mere deliverance of the dance from the shackles of the past." Her aim, says Sorell, was nothing less than "the deliverance of humanity, and dance was a means to this end."

Naturally, such lofty aims could not easily be achieved by her followers. For all her ambitions, Duncan left no school, no established set of techniques; she left nothing but the memory of her own inspired performances and bold experiments in body movement. Few of her students—and few other dancers, for that matter—have had the genius to look within themselves, as she did, define their internal feelings, and then translate those feelings into dances.

Duncan proved it was possible. Dancers coming after her could not ignore her goal: "To express the truth of my being in gestures and movement." Even the ballet she despised has changed, responding to her discoveries. The great Michel Fokine was one of the first dancemasters to learn from Duncan's lyrical, barefoot creations. He abandoned the stiff format of the traditional ballet to produce such brilliant dances as *The Firebird* (1910) and *Petrouchka* (1911), set to the explosive music of modern composer Igor Stravinsky. Inspired by Duncan, these works of the Ballets Russes helped push dance out of its fairy-tale world and into the 20th century.

Ruth St. Denis (1878–1968), a highly influential modern dancer and choreographer, dances one of the Egyptian-flavored works for which she was celebrated. She called Duncan an "indescribable genius" who "evoked visions of the morning of the world."

Martha Graham (b. 1893), one of the legends of 20th-century dance, performs Cave of the Heart *in 1946. Graham was strongly influenced by Duncan's pioneering work, particularly in her use of contemporary social and political themes.*

But most of all, Duncan is remembered as the mother of *modern* dance. It was she who paved the way for the great dancers of our era: Ruth St. Denis, Merce Cunningham, Martha Graham, Paul Taylor, and Twyla Tharp, to name just a few of the Americans. Duncan showed them that they could do much more than merely illustrate a story, demonstrating how they could let their imaginations play over every as-

pect of life—and how they could go beyond the strictly regulated ballet steps to create *unique* movements that would reflect a world grown increasingly complicated. After Duncan, dances could be about anything—two world wars, the rise of factories, even the promise of the American dream.

Beyond what she gave to dance, Duncan was an original, a visionary who always stuck to her ideals. The loose, flowing clothing she popularized brought new grace and freedom to women who had been bound up in the painful corsets of the 19th century. More important, her defiance of convention, her tenacious insistence on being herself, served as a model of liberation for millions of women all over the world. Ignoring all contemporary guidelines for "proper" behavior, she openly practiced what was then called "free love," raising with undisguised pride and affection the children she had borne outside marriage. Following her example, many women of her time began to see health, independence, and self-fulfillment as legitimate, obtainable goals.

Duncan always aroused intense controversy. Some saw her as a goddess, others as an immoral exhibitionist. Few, however, could deny that she was one of the greatest performing artists in American theatrical history. Larger than life, a legendary figure of her era, she will be long remembered as a courageous individualist who gave the world a new vision of beauty and strength.

Duncan's exuberant grace is captured in a watercolor sketch by Auguste Rodin. "Her art," said the great French sculptor, "has influenced my work more than any other inspiration. Sometimes I think she is the greatest woman the world has ever known."

FURTHER READING

Anderson, Jack. *Dance*. New York: Newsweek Books, 1974.

Blair, Fredrika. *Isadora: Portrait of the Artist as a Woman*. New York: McGraw-Hill, 1986.

Coe, Robert. *Dance in America*. New York: Dutton, 1985.

Duncan, Isadora. *The Art of the Dance*. Edited by Sheldon Cheney. New York: Theater Arts Books, 1969.

———. *My Life*. New York: Liveright, 1955.

Fonteyn, Margot. *The Magic of Dance*. New York: Knopf, 1979.

MacDougal, Allan Ross. *Isadora: A Revolutionary in Art and Love*. New York: Thomas Nelson, 1960.

McVay, Gordon. *Isadora & Esenin*. Ann Arbor, MI: Ardis, 1980.

Schneider, Ilya Ilyich. *Isadora Duncan: The Russian Years*. New York: Harcourt, Brace & World, 1968

Sorrel, Walter. *Dance in Its Time*. New York: Anchor Press/Doubleday, 1981.

Terry, Walter. *Isadora Duncan: Her Life, Her Art, Her Legacy*. New York: Dodd, Mead, 1963.

CHRONOLOGY

May 27, 1878	Born Angela Isadora Duncan in San Francisco
1895	Begins dancing career in Chicago and New York City
1899	Goes to London with family
1902	Gives first public theater performance, in Budapest, Hungary
1903	Goes to Greece with family
1904	Dances at Bayreuth Festival in Germany
	Meets Edward Gordon Craig
1905	Dances in St. Petersburg and Moscow
	Opens dance school in Berlin
1906	Gives birth to daughter, Deirdre
1908	Ends relationship with Craig
	Tours Russia and the United States
1909	Meets Paris Singer
1910	Gives birth to son, Patrick
1913	Deirdre and Patrick drown
1914	Duncan opens school in Paris; returns to America as World War I begins
1916	Tours South America
1917	Breaks with Singer and returns to Paris
1921	Opens dance school in Moscow
1922	Marries Russian poet Sergey Yesenin; tours United States with Yesenin
1923	Returns to Soviet Union
1925	Settles in Paris
1927	Writes autobiography, *My Life*
	Gives last concert, in Paris
Sept. 14, 1927	Dies in automobile accident

INDEX

INDEX

PICTURE CREDITS

Ruth Kozodoy, an editor and art historian, holds a Ph.D. from Columbia University. The author of *The Book of Jewish Holidays*, she is married and has three children.

Matina S. Horner is president of Radcliffe College and associate professor of psychology and social relations at Harvard University. She is best known for her studies of women's motivation, achievement, and personality development. Dr. Horner serves on several national boards and advisory councils, including those of the National Science Foundation, Time Inc., and the Women's Research and Education Institute. She earned her B. A. from Bryn Mawr College and Ph.D. from the University of Michigan, and holds honorary degrees from many colleges and universities, including Mount Holyoke, Smith, Tufts, and the University of Pennsylvania.